Writing Because
We Love To

Writing Because We Love To

Homeschoolers at Work

Susannah Sheffer

Foreword by Glenda L. Bissex

BOYNTON/COOK
HEINEMANN
Portsmouth, NH

Boynton/Cook Publishers, Inc.
A Subsidiary of
Heinemann Educational Books, Inc.
361 Hanover Street, Portsmouth, NH 03801
Offices and agents throughout the world

The following have generously given permission to use quotations
from copyrighted works:
Page 86: From *Rose, Where Did You Get That Red?* by Kenneth Koch.
Copyright © 1973 by Kenneth Koch.
Reprinted by permission of Random House, Inc.

Every effort has been made to contact the copyright holders and
students for permission to reprint borrowed material. We regret any
oversights that may have occurred and would be happy to rectify
them in future printing of this work.

Library of Congress Cataloging-in-Publication Data
Sheffer, Susannah, 1964–
    Writing because we love to : homeschoolers at work / by
Susannah Sheffer.
      p. cm.
    Includes bibliographical references.
    ISBN 0–86709–301–3
    1. Creative writing (Elementary education) 2. Home schooling—
United States.   3. Children's writings, American.
I. Title.
LB 1576.S3448   1992
649'.68—dc20   91–46813
                                        CIP

Designed by Jenny Jensen Greenleaf.
Printed in the United States of America.
92 93 94 95 96 9 8 7 6 5 4 3 2 1

As a craft [writing is] acquired through the apprentice system, but you choose your own teachers.

MARGARET ATWOOD

For Aaron, with love
and the last lines of "Two Tramps in Mud Time"

Contents

Foreword   xi

Acknowledgments   xv

Introduction: The Apprenticeship Model   1

1 · Choosing Teachers   11

2 · Using Teachers, Using Readers   25

3 · The Writing Culture   47

4 · Writing Until You Know   67

5 · Experiments and Inspired Moments   83

6 · Tools of the Trade   97

7 · Blocks and Periods of Not Writing   105

Epilogue: Devotion to the Work   115

Notes   121

Foreword

These experiences of an unusual teacher and her unusual students challenge conventional wisdom and practice while exploring remarkable possibilities in teaching writing. Susannah Sheffer teaches without a classroom; the young writers who choose to apprentice themselves to her are not under the external constraints of assignments and deadlines. What makes this apprenticeship work is their mutual commitment to writing. While she discusses issues like topic choice and how and when to respond—issues anyone who works with writers confronts—she is not proposing another program for teaching writing. Instead, her teaching moments and reflections offer insights and pose questions that programs do not. And their implications extend beyond the teaching of writing.

Looking over her shoulder as she dialogues with students, largely through letters, and as she reflects on how to respond to particular pieces of writing and particular children, we experience what teaching is like when it honors the diversity of ways people learn and write. "One of the most fascinating things about writing," she says, "is the many ways people do it." So often teaching is based on assumptions about how "everyone" learns. The larger the classes, the harder it is for teachers to see individual differences as anything but hindrances to their teaching.

As a writer who teaches writing, Sheffer is alert to the overgeneralizations and dogmas that can stifle young writers and blind teachers to the diverse ways in which writers of all ages actually work. While the process writing approach has punctured the dogma of "know what you want to write before you write it," other questionable rules remain and new ones are always ready to fill in the places of those we have cleared away. Sheffer questions the dictum of "write only what you know" and the admonition not to take dictation lest it discourage young children from taking charge of their own writing. She questions these principles because the young writers with whom she works do: Vita and Andrea insist that dictated stories are "written" by the teller not by the scribe, and Chelsea writes well about distant lands and imagined events. On the other hand, a ten-year-old boy is liberated from repeating fantastical adventure stories by the realization that he can write about his own life. When we listen to children, we often find conventional wisdom is challenged, and as long as we keep listening to them, we cannot simply substitute new rules for old ones.

Instead of rules, Sheffer offers us exemplars—particular teaching events which we can learn from by calling them to mind in other situations, to help us think about those situations and decide what to do. Her book shows us a teacher, facing the pedagogical questions any writing teacher does, who continues to free herself from dogma about teaching writing. And how does she teach out there on a limb, unsupported by rules? By trusting her students' self-knowledge, by asking them questions so she can learn from their learning, by reflecting on her own experiences as a writer and learner, and by following her intuitions but not without evaluating carefully where they have led.

She suggests that students decide how to use their teachers rather than teachers taking all the responsibility for and control of teaching. What she shows us, as we see her teaching, is another role for teachers, one in which they do not have to know all the answers, including how to teach every student. This should be reassuring to teachers and to parents alike. Her experiences have challenged me to explore more profoundly what it means to trust my students as learners and to see myself as vested with authority by them rather than by the academic system.

Sheffer suggests that children choose their own teachers, not as an indulgence but as experience in "one of the central tasks of growing up"—indeed of continuing to grow all the rest of our lives. On this notion she includes a wonderful quote from that great learner John Holt:

One might say that one of our important life tasks was to find our true teachers, to make our own university, and we can say of education that it is a process that ought to help us get along better at doing this. Certainly to find one of one's own teachers, someone from whom we think we can learn something really important, is one of the really great pleasures of life.

Imagine the energy of students released to choose their own teachers! Imagine the joy of teachers surrounded by students who have chosen to learn from them! Such a revolution in schools where so much is compulsory—from the students' presence at a particular place to how they use their time and with whom—boggles the mind. But Sheffer' sharing of her microcosmic revolution enables us to see in specific detail what this might mean for individual teachers and students and to contemplate its implications on a larger scale.

It's easy for schools, especially large ones, to manage students as interchangeable units and teachers as interchangeable: teachers should be able to teach any student, and students should be able to learn equally from any teacher. Yet a moment's reflection on our own experiences as learners and teachers tells us this is not so. When students have choices, usually in high school or college, guidance counselors and academic advisors talk in terms of courses though students themselves often have a truer instinct that what they are seeking and choosing among are teachers. Those who have proven to be, for our particular needs, true teachers are the ones we remember long after graduation (along with those who have positively harmed our learning).

"Teacher," however, has a broader meaning than the one usually designated by schools. When learners, which can include all of us, have access to a wide range of books—not one anonymous text book—then we are choosing our teachers. We also learn from friends who are particularly knowledgeable about things we want to know and who may speak more our language than formal teachers do. And then there are our inner teachers who are confirmed when outer teachers, like Susannah Sheffer, trust our self-knowledge and choices, trust us even to learn from mistaken choices.

Writing Because We Love To is about finding and trusting the motivation that guides and energizes learning from within, not the kind of "motivation" that is pumped into students to move them toward other people's goals, the phony, temporary motivation hype of educational promoters. It is about commitment—about how commitment directs learning. We may learn obediently what others say we should, but we commit ourselves to what we feel is important for us, for our lives, which no school district or state or national curriculum can dictate. And so this is a book to make us—teachers, parents, students—reflect on what learning and teaching truly are and how we can provide conditions (not regulations) to nourish both in our homes and in our schools.

Not all children care as much about learning to write better as do the children we meet in this book, but for each of us—child and adult alike—there is something we want to do better and for which we seek our own teachers. In that sense, *Writing Because We Love To* is about all of us during the whole course of our lives.

GLENDA L. BISSEX

Acknowledgments

I am grateful to this book's first readers and teachers—Suzanne E. Berger, Aaron Falbel, Katherine McAlpine, and Nancy Wallace—for responding in ways that helped me see what the book needed and made me want to get right to work, and to its editor, Peter Stillman, who knows how to get a book out of a writer.

I thank the young people described in these pages for trusting me with their work, answering my many questions, and allowing me to write about them here. I admire their insight, dedication, and skill tremendously, and with whatever power I may have to do it, I give them a hearty welcome into the writing culture:

Heidi Barnes, Amanda Bergson-Shilcock, Ami Carnahan, Chelsea Chapman, Serena Gingold, Kim Kopel, Dory Lerew, Kaila Morris, Tabitha Mountjoy, Ehren Nagel, Mika Perrine, Emma Roberts, Jennifer Ryan, Ariel Simmons, Nathan Williamson.

INTRODUCTION

The Apprenticeship Model

In the mail today is a group of poems from Chelsea. I've been looking forward to hearing from her, because the last time she wrote she was experimenting with poems that don't rhyme, and I'm interested to see whether or not she's continuing to work with this form. I also have on my desk a letter from Jenny, who has asked me what adult writers do when they can't think of an idea for a story. I'm thinking of how to describe what I do in that situation, and of where Jenny can read about what other writers do.

Chelsea and Jenny are two of the young people who send me their writing and ask me to comment on it. As I write this, there are about five or six young people whom I hear from regularly, a few I haven't heard from in a while but might hear from again, and two or three who wrote only once and seem to have been satisfied with that. Some have sent their work (poems, stories, essays) with only a brief note attached; others regularly include long letters about writing and about other parts of their lives. Some have become close friends of mine; others I know only through the work they send. Their ages range from ten to fifteen, and they come from all over the country.

They have in common the fact that they do not attend a conventional school; they are "self-educators," as one puts it (home-schoolers or home educators are the common terms). Some spend time on what we think of as formal schoolwork; others spend little

1

or no time engaged in schoolwork as such. I know that the writing they send me is not in response to assignments from their parents or in conjunction with a prescribed curriculum. It is, so to speak, their own work. Some share their work with their parents regularly; others do not.

Three years ago I ran a small notice in *Growing Without Schooling*, the magazine about home education of which I am editor, that said, "I'd like to offer to read and comment on the writing of young *GWS* readers. This could be a one-time thing or an ongoing arrangement, depending on what you're looking for. My only rule is that you already enjoy writing—I don't want to try to 'motivate' someone who isn't genuinely interested in writing right now."

When I ran that notice I had already been reading and commenting on the work of two young writers whom I knew personally. One lived several hours away, and we worked out a system of twice-weekly telephone calls during which we would discuss her current work. I supplemented these calls with comments sent through the mail. After a while I began to see that although I did not have access to one regular group of children close by, I had found a way to work with young writers that did not depend on their being able to meet with me (or each other) regularly. I ran the notice in *GWS* because I wanted to let other young people know that I was available for this kind of help. I hoped to hear from kids I hadn't known about before, and I thought that such a notice would attract those kids who were, for whatever reasons of their own, ready to make use of such an offer. I was interested to see how they would respond and what the responses would reveal about their writing lives and their interest in finding a teacher outside their own families. Indeed, the kids' letters *about* their work have turned out to be as interesting as the work itself.

After the first few young people responded, I began to speak at conferences and workshops about my work with them. When parents who had heard me speak told their children about it, a few more wrote to me as well.

A word or two about the population these kids come from is in order here. The homeschooling population is, at the time of this writing, mostly (though not exclusively) a middle-class, white population. It might be more accurate to say that the families come from middle-class *backgrounds* but have, in many cases, now chosen to live on fairly little money. The parents' levels of schooling vary more than many people imagine; one does not have to have a teaching certificate, or even a college degree, in order to be a successful homeschooling parent. Moreover, though these parents support their kids' efforts in a general sense, it is not always the case that they themselves are particularly devoted to the specific activities that the kids have chosen. Not all the kids in this book have parents who are serious writers, in other words.

The portion of the homeschooling population that reads *GWS* tends to be more liberal politically than the whole (although this too varies) and, most significant, tends to favor self-directed learning over following a curriculum. The kids I'm discussing here are especially able to direct their own educations, to decide when to do what and how much adult involvement they would like.

The greatest diversity in the handful of kids I have been working with is probably geographical. Amanda's life in suburban Philadelphia is very different from Chelsea's in Alaska or Tabitha's in rural Missouri. Having grown up in New York City, I have been interested to see young writers growing and flourishing in many different places, against many different kinds of landscapes and daily lives.

In one important respect, the kids I have worked with so far have been alike: almost all have been girls. I don't entirely understand why this has been so. Some people have suggested to me that perhaps girls, at these ages, are more likely to be interested in writing than boys are, since traditional female socialization favors just this sort of quiet, introspective activity during these years. There may be something to this, but homeschoolers don't tend to be particularly vulnerable to the prevailing norms of their peer group in other respects, so I don't know why they should be in this one. Also, many boys at just these ages write to *Growing Without Schooling* and are published in it, and I have seen plenty of work by boys in collections of homeschooled student writing, so boys at the same age, from the same population, do in fact write.

Another possible explanation for my apprentices' uniformity in this regard may be that a woman offering to help young writers is more likely to attract girls than boys. I suspect there is some truth in this classic role-model theory because personal friendship so often arises out of the mentor-apprentice relationship, and has indeed arisen between me and several of my apprentices. But I don't mean to say that children can learn only from people of their own gender. I had important male teachers during my own childhood and adolescence, and in fact these girls do as well, in other areas of their lives.

So despite these theories I cannot offer any definitive explanation of why most of the kids who have so far taken me up on my offer have been girls. Part of it may truly be coincidence.

Some people ask what it is like to work with young writers through the mail instead of in person. The method does have its limitations. I can't always tell how my comments have affected the writers. Did I say too much at once? Should I have explained that point more thoroughly? Some of the natural feedback that is present during face-to-face interactions is missing. But sometimes I think that this limitation has a positive side, too. Using the mail gives my work with the children a particular pace, one that allows me time to think about their writing, for however long I need to, before responding to it, and allows them time to digest my comments and to determine the intervals between our interactions. They can use me frequently, as they are likely to when they are working hard at something that they want to finish soon, or they can let long periods elapse between our letters.

In addition to the lack of immediate feedback, another limitation inherent in this kind of work is that I only know what the young people tell me, through their work and their letters about that work. When I began to have more specific questions about how they went about their work, I arranged to talk to several of them on the telephone. But unlike others who are trying to learn about how particular children learn and work, I am unable to see these young people regularly, to enjoy that immersion in their lives that classroom teachers, or parents writing about their own children, enjoy as a matter of course.

But this, too, may have its benefits. I think children may sometimes appreciate having a relationship with an adult that is *not* based on years of familiarity, that doesn't come complete with old assumptions and memories. In the course of my work at *Growing Without Schooling*, I hear from hundreds of parents who write about their children. These letters are full of fascinating observations, and they have an important place in the literature about how children learn. One unexpected reward that has come from working with these young writers, however, has been the chance to hear from the young people directly, and to respond to them directly. I enjoy, sometimes, *not* knowing about the children's early development from their parents' perspective (for example), but rather allowing the children to present themselves and their work to me on their own terms.

Before making my offer to these kids, I already had many reasons for believing that I wanted to teach by making myself available to young people who would come to me voluntarily and who would decide in what ways and how often they wanted to make use of me, rather than by working in a classroom. I was already quite familiar with home education, having corresponded with the educator John Holt, one of its chief advocates, for several years and then having assumed editorship of *Growing Without Schooling,* the magazine he founded, after his death in 1985. I believed that young people could and ought to be able to make choices about their education and was interested in what happened under such circumstances. I wanted to learn about kids who wrote not because writing was a required subject but because they had discovered for themselves its uses and its importance.

Neither by circumstance nor philosophy could I imagine myself teaching full-time. I was busy with my own writing and editorial work, and had come to believe, for reasons that will become clearer as I go along, that teaching is best done as an adjunct to a life of activity, of actually doing whatever it is one wants to teach. I agreed with Frank Smith, who writes in his book *Insult to Intelligence,* "We learn by apprenticing ourselves to people who practice what they teach."[1] Smith believes it is crucial that writing teachers write, math teachers do math, and so on. In my experience with children and teenagers, I found that they naturally expected to learn from people who did things. The young people I've worked with have known me as a writer, seen what I've written, and in some cases seen me at work writing it. They see me as a writer who might be able to teach rather than as a writing teacher, a difference that has come to seem to me crucial, and that I will explore in greater depth here.

Liking Smith's phrase, I now call the young people I work with my writing apprentices, a phrase they themselves seem to like. I first got the idea that apprenticeship could apply to activities other than crafts or strictly physical skills from the British theoretical physicist David Deutsch, who wrote in an early issue of *GWS,*

What happens if a child of (say) 12 acquires a keen interest in fundamental physics? . . . [I]f the interest persists he will probably soon begin to exhaust the rewards of learning single-handedly from books and even such things as Open University broadcasts. The point here is not that he will run out of facts to learn: he will not. The point is that factual knowledge from such sources constitutes only part of what a physicist needs to know. The more important part is a complex set of attitudes and ideas concerning, for example, the recognition of what constitutes a physics problem, how one goes about solving it, and what might be acceptable as a solution. One can learn such things in only one way: by participating in the physics culture.[2]

Deutsch goes on to outline the apprenticeship model that he imagines following from the child's desire to participate in the physics culture. The child, "who had already been attracted, for reasons of his own," to participation in the physics culture, would seek Deutsch's help in exploring the questions about physics that had intrigued him. The child, in other words, would already have some work of his own with which he thought Deutsch could be helpful.

Deutsch, the experienced physicist, would in turn have his own work, his research topics, and that work could be broken down into smaller tasks with which the apprentice could help. One of the important aspects of Deutsch's model is that it is mutually satisfying to the apprentice and the teacher. He describes the ways in which the apprentice would be "truly productive from the beginning," as helpful to Deutsch (though in different ways) as Deutsch is to the apprentice. After time, the apprentice "would begin to think like a physicist as he unconsciously assimilated inexplicit knowledge simply by observing a physicist solving problems. He would begin to enjoy more and more the inner rewards of doing physics. At the same time he would become steadily more useful to me in an ever wider range of sub-tasks."

Much of what Deutsch describes seems possible in a writing apprenticeship: the participating in the writing culture, the learning how to think like a writer. But how the mutuality can manifest itself in a writing apprenticeship may be less obvious, since in writing there's no clear point at which it is appropriate for the apprentice to take over the task at hand. I don't delegate my own tasks to my apprentices in the way that Deutsch imagines he would, simply because the nature of the work doesn't lend itself to doing so in the same way. I may on occasion involve one of my apprentices directly in my work by asking her to read what I've written. I certainly tell the kids about my work—problems I'm struggling with, decisions I've made. When kids help out in my office, as local homeschoolers do occasionally and as one of the kids in this book was able to do when she came for a visit, the arrangement is closest to what Deutsch describes: I delegate several of the tasks involved in putting out the magazine, and the kids get to feel a direct connection between their help and the larger goal. They learn while being genuinely useful.

The kind of writing apprenticeship I will explore in the following pages is not of this sort, however. The kids are not working for me in the way that a classic apprentice works for a master. Why then do I persist in characterizing these kids as apprentices, when such a crucial element of the apprenticeship model is missing? Perhaps I might more accurately call them students.

The appeal of the apprenticeship model, for me, and why it seems to describe these kids and our arrangement better than simply "student," is twofold: it implies a rootedness in real-world as opposed to classroom activities, and it draws attention to the active decision that the young people have made to learn from me. When we think of apprenticeships for young people in other areas of adult work, we think of them as ways to get young people out of the classroom and into the working world, and that's the part that seems to fit the experience of the kids with whom I'm working. Furthermore, I'm interested in the idea of *apprenticing oneself* to someone else, in the active choice that that implies (and that my reading of the Margaret Atwood quote that is this book's epigraph implies as well). I will explore the idea of apprenticeship as active choice further in the next chapter.

Even when my apprentices are not helping me as directly as traditional apprentices help mentors, they are giving me something useful and important. I thought about this when a woman called my office to ask about apprenticeships. "Not for my children," she said. "For me." She said that she knows a little bit about piano tuning and wants to learn more, but what stops her from trying to apprentice herself to an experienced piano tuner is her fear that it would be purely selfish. "What would be in it for the experienced apiano tuner?" she wondered.

Some people may take on apprentices simply because they feel an obligation to pass on what they know, or to give to others the kind of help that was once given to them. Certainly that's part of my motivation; I want to pass on what I know, share what I love, and also give some things I *wasn't* given but would like to have been offered. But beyond this, I'm always amazed at how much *is* in fact in it for the experienced piano tuner, or physicist, or writer. Maverick surgeon Bernie Siegel says, "We teach what we want to learn." My writing apprentices are teaching me about how young people grow as writers under a particular set of circumstances, and these circumstances are more like those under which I and other adult writers work than they are like the circumstances of the classroom. My apprentices are working at writing without the benefit or the limitation (depending on your perspective) of a formal curriculum. They don't have to write on assigned topics, or at particular times of the day, or for specific teachers or audiences (except, as we will see, when they choose to do so). Because they are writing under what we might call adult, or real-world, conditions, they help me think about my own writing in ways that children in classrooms, through no fault of their own, could not. I suspect it works the other way, too: our similar circumstances probably make my experience more useful to my apprentices than it would otherwise be. My relationship with them is certainly more collegial than teacher-student relationships tend to be.

Not much of the literature about children's writing development has looked at how writing develops under the circumstances I have described. For what reasons do children write, if writing is not a required subject? What kind of help do they seek out, if they have the opportunity to choose who their teachers will be and what they will learn from those teachers? What do they do when they reach a difficult point in their work?

Readers unfamiliar with home education may find it difficult to imagine how children who are not given direct instruction learn the basic, or technical, skills of writing (or reading, for that matter) that enable them to get to the point at which I come in. Never mind how they write stories or poems; how have they learned to form letters, to spell, to punctuate? The literature about home education is full of answers to this question, full of stories about how children become literate without formal instruction. Kim, to whom I will be referring regularly, describes her early reading and writing experiences as follows:

> I learned to write when I was between the ages of 3 and 4;
> I wanted to be able to write, so I asked people (Mom and Dad

and other relatives and friends) how to make the letters of the alphabet. As soon as I could form the letters, I began writing letters to people; I would decide what I wanted to say, and then ask people how to spell the words. In this way, I learned correct spelling and grammar, and gained a knowledge of letters and words that later made it possible for me to learn to read. When I was about 10 I began keeping a diary, which I'm still writing in now, and at the same time I also began writing stories. . . .

I learned to read pretty much the same way I learned to write, a few years later. I remember being read to a lot, which I really enjoyed, and wanting to be able to read. I learned to read from being read to, being answered when I asked, "What does that say?" (which was quite frequently), and writing, which helped me to recognize words. Most of all, I learned to read (and write, and do everything I know how to do) because I wanted to be able to. I never used any workbooks, flashcards, etc. when I was learning to read or write.

Of course, not all homeschooled children learn to read and write in just this way, or at this age; one of the chief characteristics of this alternative is the diversity of approach that it allows. Readers seeking other such stories, or a more detailed discussion of how homeschooling works, can turn to the many books and articles that are available. For my purposes, let it suffice to say that the kids I work with *have* acquired basic facility with written language by the time they come to me, although there are naturally all sorts of stylistic and typographical conventions that they have yet to learn. Readers should bear in mind, too, that my focus is on kids for whom writing is a major love and interest. It's natural that these are the kids who would respond to an offer such as mine, so in one sense it's simply by default that they are ones I've come to know the best. But I'm also interested in them as a particular group, both selfishly (because they help me understand myself and my work) and because I am interested in the notion of "coming to a vocation," as educational critic Herbert Kohl calls it. Why have these young people chosen to devote themselves to writing? (I don't mean that they have devoted themselves to writing exclusively, or to the same degree in each case, but that they write out of devotion more than out of obligation.) How does that devotion manifest itself? What can we learn from them about how a vocation is best served?

Though the children in this book are working under conditions that are very different from the classroom's, I would like to think that their stories will be of use to classroom teachers. Teachers may come away from this book with new ideas about what children are capable of or thoughts about how to bring more of the real-world writing culture into the classroom (and perhaps to get children into apprenticeship situations outside the classroom as well). The kids' descriptions of how they work best may contain information that teachers can put to use in their classrooms. I spoke with one teacher about this book's discussion of how kids use periods of not writing, for example, and he told me that he could imagine teachers working that understanding into their overall plan for the year by allowing for periods of writing and periods of time away from writing. Many other such applications may be possible.

I also imagine that parents—homeschooling or not—will come away with ideas about how to respond to their children's writing and how to make their own writing lives accessible. Young writers may find kindred spirits in these pages and discover that reading about others like themselves is one way of feeling a part of the writing culture. Adult writers may find the book an invitation to reflect on their own writing development.

More than anything else, I hope readers will come away with an appreciation of the competence young people can achieve and the insight and reflection of which they are capable. This book is not about techniques as much as it is about the respect and seriousness that can characterize kids' attitudes toward their work and adults' attitudes toward children. It is about the conditions under which these attitudes are likely to grow, and about what happens when they are present. We can all learn from these writers who are writing because they love to rather than because they have to, and who have the time and the opportunity to figure out what best serves their work.

ONE

Choosing Teachers

"I don't mind having teachers at all," fourteen-year-old Kim wrote to me, "but only when I want them, and only the teachers I choose." A year earlier Kim had been one of the first young people to respond to my offer in *Growing Without Schooling.* At that time she was writing a long fictional story, and she asked me to comment on the first chapter. Soon afterward, though, Kim turned her attention to a new project. She conceived the idea of writing a journal, meant for others to read, about her education. She wanted people to understand what a self-educated teenager does all day, how she learns what she wants to know, and what she believes about education in general. Because of this project, which has dominated Kim's writing life for most of the time we've been working together, and because of our mutual interest in educational issues, Kim often writes to me about learning and teaching.

When she wrote that she didn't mind having teachers as long as she could choose them, we had been talking about how young people in school are assigned teachers from whom they must learn, (or try to learn), whether they want to or not. Kim has several teachers in her life—her parents, naturally, and the people outside the family with whom she has studied weaving, Irish dance, and, most recently, choral singing. But because she has never been to school, she has no experience with teachers whom she hasn't chosen for herself. Of course, she didn't choose her parents, and they,

11

indeed, are often her teachers. But their philosophy of education is such that when it comes to academic subjects they are only her teachers when she wants or asks them to be, although they do a great deal of inadvertent teaching in the course of their daily lives. They read, use numbers, and so on, and Kim, like all young people, learns from their example. But Kim's parents don't set out to teach her something that she hasn't yet decided she wants to learn. Instead, they respond to Kim when and in the ways that she asks them to. So in that sense she chooses them as well.

To most of us, the idea of school-aged children and teenagers choosing the people from whom they will learn, especially from whom they will learn "basic" or academic subjects, seems unusual and even frightening. Would they choose wisely? Why would they even want teachers enough to go looking for them? What, for that matter, is so bad about being assigned teachers?

When I was in ninth grade I met with my English teacher to discuss the poems I was planning to enter in a national contest. As this teacher spoke about possible revisions of the poems, she repeatedly made comments like, "I know what you were thinking of when you wrote this line," and "When you write, you . . . " I vividly remember feeling confused and mystified. It seemed to me that this teacher was telling me things about my writing that she could not possibly know and with which I could not agree. I didn't know how to tell her that I was not, in fact, thinking what she told me I had been thinking, and that I did not always write by the processes by which she was sure I wrote.

This had happened before. English teachers in school, speaking to me or to the class as a whole, had often said things about writing that directly contradicted my own experience. This might not have bothered me if they had not talked as though their ways were the only ways, or if they had seemed to be speaking from their own experience as writers. But I had never seen any writing by my English teachers, and never got the sense that they produced any. I didn't have the feeling that I now have in writing workshops of receiving criticism from someone who is clearly plying the same trade.

Looking back on it now, it strikes me that these well-meaning teachers confused what they observed as readers with what they imagined the writer had consciously intended. Often their comments seemed to assume that the features of a poem or story that they had been trained as English teachers to detect and explain were conscious techniques that the writers had employed during the writing. I was never so sure of this. When teachers said, in so many words, that the writer had meant this or intended that, I would mutter to myself, "How do you know?" This skepticism was fed directly by my experience with what happened when the teachers' critical method was applied to my own work. If they couldn't accurately guess at or describe what had been going on in my head when I wrote, how could I trust their assertions about the writers we read?

I see now that the English teachers were speaking primarily as readers, rather than as writers. They were talking about what they saw in the work, but confusing the issue by making it seem as though they could see into the mind of the writer as well. If I had understood this distinction, things might have been easier for me. I might not have tried to learn about writing from these particular teachers in the first place. But writing *was* part of the English curriculum, and, as I've described, the teachers did take it upon themselves to help me with my writing, so I wasn't immediately able to understand why I was so rattled when they talked authoritatively about ways of writing that were not the ways in which I wrote. In time, though, and without quite realizing that I was doing it, I began to look for other teachers.

I discovered the *Writers at Work* interview series published by the *Paris Review*, and soon found, in those interviews, nuggets of confirmation of my own writing experience. When these nuggets contradicted what my English teachers had said, I decided—emphatically if not quite consciously—to believe the writers in the interviews instead.

My English teachers were assigned to me; the writers in the *Writers at Work* series were not. Structurally, the English teachers were the teachers from whom I was supposed to learn. I didn't dare challenge their real and imagined power by offering a contradictory view of how people write, although perhaps I should have. I attempted to make sense of the disparity and reconcile the contradiction quietly, by myself. But this felt furtive, defiant. Like Kim, I wanted to be able to choose my teachers, but unlike Kim I had to do this on the sly, in defiance of the people I was supposed to think of as teachers. I wasted time on guilt and justification, time that Kim and the other young writers I work with do not have to waste. They have to find their teachers just as I did, but they can do this without feeling that the very act of doing it makes them rebels.

In an unpublished manuscript called "Notes for a Talk to Students," the late educator John Holt writes:

> In the past 28 years at least I've been the president of a university, and quite a good one. It has a student body of one—namely, me. The faculty of the university is made up of all the people from whom I think I can learn something that I think is important to me in terms of my own life's goals, something, to use Kropotkin's words, that would help me understand better what kind of world I want, what kind of life I want to live in it, the ways in which I can work to make such a world and life, and the things I need to know in order to do that—or simply the things that will heighten my pleasure and excitement in living. When I find such a person, I quickly put him on my faculty. He doesn't know it. There are no salaries in my university. Some of the faculty of my university are alive, some are dead; some are known to me, some close friends, some are people I have yet to meet. I'm constantly hiring and firing on my faculty; there is no tenure in my university. Some of the people who at one time in my life were very important teachers to me no longer are. Perhaps I now see the world differently, no longer agree with what they told me. Perhaps I've simply absorbed what they had to tell me, and moved on. Others of my teachers in the past are my teachers still.
>
> One might say that one of our important life tasks was to find our true teachers, to make our own university, and we can say of education that it is a process that ought to help us get better at doing this. Certainly to find one of one's own teachers, someone from whom we think we can learn something really important, is one of the really great pleasures of life.

Holt's university turns the traditional model of education inside out. Instead of being *assigned* to teachers, students *seek out* people from whom they want to learn. This is the university that the young people I work with attend. If I am their teacher, it is because they have made me so. If I stop being useful to them, they can look for someone else.

The difference between choosing teachers and having teachers assigned to us is the difference between investing someone with authority and having that authority used on, or held over, us. The teachers that John Holt put on his "faculty" were people in whom he had invested authority; *he* had decided that he could learn something from them. When we speak of apprenticeship, we may say that a teacher has *taken on* an apprentice, focusing on the element of choice on the teacher's part (I had no obligation to help young writers until I specifically decided to take them on). But we also say that people *apprentice themselves* to experienced practitioners, referring to the active choice that the learner makes. We apprentice ourselves to people when we decide we can learn from them. This connotation of choice in both uses of the word "apprentice" is what invites me to use it in this discussion, as I said in the introduction.

In this sense of the word, we can apprentice ourselves to people who don't even know we've done it (as Holt describes). For example, fourteen-year-old Amanda said to me, "I think I've been reading like a writer more and more lately. When I read I think about what the author has done and whether I could do that. I guess I must have been reading like a writer all along, subconsciously, or I wouldn't have learned how to write correctly. But now I'm doing it consciously." Just as I did at her age, Amanda apprentices herself to writers she has never met. She invests them with authority and engages in the active business of learning from them. Naturally, this kind of apprenticeship relationship is not the same as the one Amanda has with me or with other people she knows personally, but it's an apprenticeship relationship nonetheless.

Students in school have not necessarily invested their teachers with authority. They haven't made these adults into teachers in the way that they would be able to if they could choose (and refuse) them. Again, the difference is in who does the deciding. Do I decide that I have something to learn from you, or do you decide that you have something to teach me?

Traditionally, we give children teachers and expect them to learn from them. Some do, by happy coincidence; some children find that the teachers who are assigned to them *are* people from whom they can learn. They are lucky, although even they miss out on the challenge of actively seeking out teachers, and may be at a loss when an institution stops providing them. But others don't learn from the teachers they are given—don't, in any real sense, consider those people their teachers—and so conclude that they can't learn at all, or that learning is no fun, or that there's something wrong with them for learning more from people outside school than from people in it. In *The Question Is College*, Herbert Kohl describes two young people who had had very difficult school careers. "They had no apparent learning problems," Kohl writes. "They just didn't want to learn from the people who were assigned to teach them."[3] How do we respond to such young people? How do we view that refusal?

Too often, instead of being recognized as one of the central tasks of growing up, finding teachers becomes an extra-curricular activity, as it was for me when I read *Writers at Work* only after completing my assigned English homework, or an activity we can begin only when we leave school. "Learning after college was the most exciting of all, when I could finally pursue my own curriculum," writes the writer and researcher Donald Graves as he describes his life's teachers. "When I had a chance to set up my own teachers for learning my way, the learning/teaching events began to multiply."[4] Why should Graves have had to wait until he was out of college, in his twenties, to be able to "set up his own teachers," to pursue his own curriculum? What would have happened if he had had the opportunity to begin much earlier?

Unlike Donald Graves, the young writers I know haven't had to wait. They are setting up their own teachers right now, deciding who they will learn from, and when, and in what ways. This is one of the things I find most interesting about them. When do they decide that they want someone outside the family to read their writing and work with them on it? Why do they want such a teacher, if they have not been assigned that teacher or told that having one was important?

Sometimes a child sought me out initially because she had a specific question she thought I could answer. In ten-year-old Mika's first letter to me, she wrote, "The problem I often have is thinking of a plot. I'm pretty good at characters and settings, but I often have 'writer's block.' If you could give me suggestions on this point, it would really help. In the meantime, you could look over my writing and make comments and suggestions."

Sometimes the writer's first question is not about writing, but about what kind of teacher I am. Before Heidi, who at twelve was new to homeschooling, went ahead and sent me the long story about army life on which she'd been working for some time, she asked me several questions about what I offered young writers and how I worked with them. This kind of shopping around—

interviewing prospective teachers before going ahead and working with them—is something that adults can do as a matter of course but that children are seldom able to do. Often adults do this work *for* their children; they may talk to teachers of after-school classes before deciding to enroll their children, or, when possible, may even choose from among possible classroom teachers. In some cases, a child may be happy to have the parent prescreen teachers in this way. But how interesting and how direct it is when young people are given the opportunity to choose for themselves.

"I wanted someone to tell me honestly what I needed to do," said Chelsea, at fourteen, thinking back to when she had first sent me her poems, two years ago. The desire for an honest response, by which they often mean one that includes criticism or suggestions for improvement, comes up repeatedly in the kids' descriptions of what they were looking for when they began working with me. Chelsea said that her parents generally respond to her writing by saying, "That's fine; leave it the way it is," probably, she speculates, because they don't want to offend her by saying anything stronger.

Ariel, at eleven, echoed Chelsea's thoughts when she wrote, after I'd responded to the first story she sent me, "I think you mentioned things [in the story] my mother didn't because she didn't want to sound picky. That is, she'd question some things but so as not to hurt my feelings (she really wouldn't) she wouldn't question too much."

Ariel takes care to point out that although her mother might have worried that detailed criticism would hurt her daughter's feelings, such a response would not have been offended Ariel. Once kids ask us for help or response, they don't want us to handle them with kid gloves. They want us to be honest, both because our honesty implies respect for their work and because honest responses are the ones that are truly useful.

Thirteen-year-old Ami made this clear when she sent me a long story and said in the accompanying letter, "I don't want your approval, but your advice and maybe even some criticism. Don't worry about hurting my feelings 'cause I'm asking for it. I'm pretty devoted to my writing and want to find ways to improve it."

It intrigued me that Ami was willing to send her work across the country to someone she didn't know at all, and that she could be so clear about what she wanted so early in our working relationship. She certainly persuaded me that she was ready for help and critical

17

response. I could see that her devotion to her writing was what made her want this criticism; having made the commitment to the work, she wanted help in doing it as well as possible. This is why, of all the comments that I made on Ami's story (many of them enthusiastic), she was most grateful for the ones I had feared were the harshest. Referring to my comments about two weak aspects of the story, Ami wrote, "*That* is what I'm looking for. . . . I like exactly how you're responding and helping me now."

Amanda, at fourteen, was similarly grateful when I pointed out one or two speech anachronisms in a story she had set in 1884. "I just got your letter an hour ago," she said to me on the telephone, "and as I read it I thought oh, this is great! This is just what I need to know." She told me that she was working on another story set in the same time period and hoped that I would point out any awkward places in that one, too.

I have just begun to work with Serena, who is now twelve, though I have known her for several years through her letters to *Growing Without Schooling* and through her family's newsletter, *Homeschoolers for Peace*, in which kids around the country write about social and political issues. (This newsletter, by the way, is an interesting example of how kids can use writing to overcome geographical isolation and to meet others with similar concerns. Serena lives in the mountains of northern California and doesn't have many neighbors, so when she and her older brother wanted to meet other kids who shared their interest in social and political activism, they used a newsletter to do it. It has turned out to be an effective way to get to know others; it has also made them stronger writers.)

Serena apparently agrees with Amanda and Ami about the value of serious criticism. After I had responded to the two stories that she sent me, she wrote:

> It really felt good to have someone outside the family criticize my work, and it was nice of you to tell me how to change it to make it more understandable. Not that my parents don't help me with this, but it was different to have someone outside my family take my work seriously enough to realize that I WANT to know what's wrong with it and how to make it better. Other people tend to say things like, "Oh! What a talented little girl!" I think they're afraid I might feel bad if someone said that it wasn't perfect. If you don't get criticism from people who really *care* that your writing is

understandable, then your writing won't get any better and will probably stay childish all your life. After I got your letter I got really excited about writing and I wrote 17½ pages of a book. It was mostly a writing exercise I did to see how long I could keep going. I followed my character through every move, which would make a long and boring book, but in doing so I felt I got to know my character much better.

We don't usually imagine that young people will be grateful to us for pointing out weak spots or places where they have failed to do what they set out to do. But these kids crave criticism because they are serious writers. They appreciate someone's pointing out the places in which they *haven't* achieved something because they have such a clear sense of what they do want to achieve.

Parents are often reluctant to criticize their children, and rightly so. But when these kids ask for responses to their writing, they are coming to adults not as children but as serious workers. Sometimes it may take a fellow worker to see that clearly, which is why I may sometimes be able to criticize where their parents hold back.

Despite how clearly eager for criticism these young people are, though, my challenge is figuring out how much to say at any one time. As I've said, because I work through the mail I can't gauge, as well as I would be able to in person, whether I've given too much for the writer to take in all at once. I often urge the writers to pick and choose from my comments, to focus on some parts now and some parts later (or never), if that's easier. And, too, I'm careful to talk about the strengths of the piece before launching into suggestions for revision.

I asked Ariel whether she ever asks her mother to critique her further. "If it's true that she wouldn't offend you by saying more, do you tell her that and ask for more?" I asked. "No," Ariel replied, "because I never want her to think I'd be helpless without her." One can want teachers and at the same time worry that those teachers will end up feeling indispensable. Somehow, it's necessary for the teacher to maintain a balance between giving too much on the one hand (making the learner feel helpless) or too little on the other (giving only praise and approval).

Another way to give too little is to speak only in generalities from which it's difficult for the learner to draw any useful advice. I remember, in fifth grade, a student teacher returning a paper to me on which she had written, "Watch your commas—you use too many." Oh dear, I thought to myself. I have a problem with commas. But how many was too many? Which particular commas in my paper were unnecessary or incorrect? How would I ever learn to apply this comma rule myself so that I would no longer have to depend on the student teacher's assessment? Looking back, I wonder whether the student teacher offered me only such a vague comment because she had too many papers to correct in a short time or because she was she was afraid of discouraging me by marking up my page too extensively. I can sympathize with both concerns, but I was more baffled by the vague admonition than I would have been by specific discussion of the commas I had actually used.

I learned the same lesson, from the other perspective, when I told Kim, early on in our work together, that she was using commas where semi-colons would be more appropriate. She didn't say anything at the time, but months later she wrote, "You once wrote something about using the semi-colon more, but I'm not too sure about where and when the semi-colon should be used, or what it even means, which makes it hard for me to use." This time I referred to specific sentences in Kim's own writing to show her where and when the semi-colon would be appropriate. Before long, she was using the semi-colon often, and correctly. Again I learned: if someone asks for help, and you agree to help, give the help in a way that is specific enough, and thorough enough, to be meaningful and useful.

Figuring out how much and what kind of help to give remains a subtle art, of course. Why do some kinds of comments from readers make us eager to get to work and others make us want to throw the whole thing in the trash? I told Ariel about my friend Nancy, who thinks that the worst kind of response a reader can give to her early drafts is, "That's fine," because it implies, to Nancy, that her reader has given up on her and doesn't even want to bother to offer detailed criticism. Ariel thought about this and then said, "Well, somewhere in here there's a happy medium." She's right. Somewhere in the relationship between learners and their chosen teachers there is a balance between too much and not enough. I have come to see that if the learners are in control of the situation, they have the best chance of striking the appropriate balance. The kids let me know how much, and what, they want from me, sometimes simply by ignoring advice that is more than they asked for or not useful at the time, sometimes by explicitly asking for particular types of comments.

A friend and I once disagreed about the extent to which we would ever put ourselves in the hands of a teacher. He said that if he had chosen a teacher he would accept that the teacher knew more about what he needed to do, and would follow the teacher's advice or instructions even if they didn't make sense or seemed unnecessary. I said that while I would sometimes follow a suggestion simply out of respect for the person who made it, if the suggestion explicitly contradicted what I thought I needed to work on, or actually seemed harmful, I wouldn't go along with it simply because I had chosen the teacher.

My stubbornness in this regard may come from my particular experiences with teachers who made suggestions that I felt were counterproductive to what I was trying to do. Still, I am glad that my apprentices feel free to reject my advice. I enjoy reading letters in which they defend a line I've suggested they cut as much as I enjoy seeing revisions in which they have taken my advice and cut the line in question. Their freedom to reject my advice means they can ask for help without worrying about what they'll do if the help turns out not to be helpful. It means that I can say what I think without always worrying that it's the wrong thing to say.

Crucial though that element is, the kids' relationship with me isn't based *only* on their ability to refuse my suggestions. The freedom that comes with choosing teachers works both ways: the kids can reject what may be harmful or unnecessary, but they can also accept and welcome what will be useful. My apprentices work more closely with me than I ever dared work with my unchosen teachers. They trust me with early drafts, ask for my honest opinion, follow up on my suggestions. This is more than I ever did. As a child in school, I didn't have enough freedom or control over the situation to take those risks.

The structure of our relationship means that the kids can accept more, and I can offer more. When Kim told me that she wasn't too familiar with poetry that didn't rhyme, I said that if she was interested I could send her some or help her try writing it, but I would understand if it wasn't her top priority. She responded, "I really liked it [when] you said I didn't have to try writing other types of poetry—you can suggest things to me, but you don't make me feel that I have to try everything. I would be interested in seeing the other kinds of poetry that you're talking about, if you'd like to send me anything."

Kim knew that she could ask to see that poetry without feeling pressured to respond to it or learn from it in any particular way. Secure in the knowledge that she is truly free to pick and choose from what I offer her, she can let me say what I want to say or suggest what I want to suggest.

People who believe that children's learning can be self-directed are sometimes confused about the difference between offering something to a young person and requiring it. If I respond to what the kids are doing and help in the ways they ask me to, rather than initiating educational activities by thinking up things for them to do or giving them assignments, what happens if they never ask about a book or material that I know would be valuable? Are they doomed to miss it because my educational beliefs forbid me from mentioning it?

This is a misunderstanding of the relationship between self-directed learners and the people in their lives. Nothing in the apprenticeship relationship forbids me from recommending books or even writing activities to the kids I work with. In fact, as I've said, it's easier for me to do this with a clear conscience than it would be if I felt the kids were under an obligation to me. Some months ago I sent Kim a book I thought she might like. I did this purely because I felt like doing it; I loved the book, it was about a writer at work, and I didn't think Kim had seen it before. But she *knew* that I didn't expect an immediate response, or indeed any response at all. She knew the spirit in which the offer was made, and that spirit is probably more characteristic of my relationship with these kids than anything else. Kim didn't say anything about the book (other than an initial thank you) for several months, but when she did, it was that the book had become one of her "all-time favorites." True, this might have happened even if I had required her to read the book, but the point is that the traditional teacher-student relationship (or, for that matter, the parent-child relationship) isn't the only one in which adults can introduce things from their own experience into the lives of young people.

Will young people who are able to choose their own teachers choose wisely? One answer is that only by being allowed to choose at all, and thus sometimes to choose poorly, can anyone develop the skills necessary to choose well. Another answer is that the better we know ourselves and our work, the better we will be at figuring out what kind of help we want. By the time these kids wrote to me, they had had years of working on their own and developing—even if not always consciously—a very clear sense of how they worked, and a strong trust in their *own* opinions. Mika, for example, had such a specific sense of what she needed to work on that she was able to ask me the precise question she posed in her first letter. And having trust in their own opinions of their work means that the kids are able to determine whether outside help is useful to them or not. If nothing I say makes sense to them or resonates with their own sense of what they need to do, they can discard it. As I've said, some kids have used my help only one time and have been free to decide that that was all they wanted.

Maybe it's no surprise that the kids who responded to my offer were all fairly close in age. We need time to develop a sure knowledge about how we work, and perhaps a certain level of maturity, before we are able to reject others' advice, especially the advice of people we like and respect. On the other hand, these abilities may have less to do with chronological age than with how long we have been involved in the particular work. A thirteen-year-old who has been writing for several years may be readier for and better able to handle criticism than a novice many years older.

Finally, my apprentices' ability to choose their teachers, to maintain control of their own work and growth, is essential to my learning from them. If they had no choice but to respond to my suggestions, I would never know which of those suggestions had been truly useful. If they were required to write every day, I wouldn't be able to learn about their actual working rhythms. Their freedom and the structure of our relationship are conditions favorable not only to their work but to my own.

TWO

Using Teachers, Using Readers

Just as we are unaccustomed to the notion of children choosing their own teachers, so are we unused to the idea that children might be able to decide how they want to use their teachers. Traditionally, teachers plan what will go on during lessons, what kind of help they will offer their students. Sometimes a teacher may say, "Do you need help with anything else?" or "Is there anything you don't understand?" thereby encouraging students to think about whether they are getting what they want from the teacher. But this is uncommon, and too often students don't know enough about themselves or their work to be able to answer those questions even when they are asked.

If you're sitting in a class that you didn't choose to take, being taught something you're not sure you wanted to learn in the first place, it may be difficult or even impossible to think about what you want from a teacher and whether you're getting it, beyond such variables as whether the teacher is "strict" or "fair" or gives a lot of work. But if you have sought out a teacher because you have already come a certain distance on your own and now think that a teacher would be helpful, you are much more likely to know what you're looking for and to be able to judge whether you've found it.

When I took my first poetry workshop, at nineteen, I hoped that what the teacher was offering would match what I was looking for, but I didn't think I would be able to do much about it if it didn't. In the years since then, as my understanding of my own work has sharpened and my confidence in my ability to determine what goes on in teacher-student interactions has grown, I have become more active. Instead of simply hoping that a teacher will give me the kind of help I want, I can actively try to get it. When the poet with whom I currently study asks our workshop what we want to do during the next few meetings, I am able to tell her. If she makes suggestions, I can see which ones I'd rather pursue, and, equally important, I can let her know.

Much of this ability comes from knowing my own priorities. When other members of the workshop suggested that we spend one session reading our work aloud, for example, I knew that that wouldn't be as useful to me as hearing their criticism, and I said so. But I wouldn't have known that if I hadn't already developed a sense of what I wanted to do and what kind of help I needed.

I encourage my apprentices to decide how they want to use me, and to let me know. Some of this is already inherent in the structure of our relationship: because they seek me out, rather than the other way around, they usually have some sense of what they want, even at the beginning (as I described in the last chapter). But they—and I—usually discover the rest of it during the course of our work. After getting my responses to one or two pieces of their writing, they may find that certain kinds of comments are more helpful than others, or that, say, they'd prefer it if I responded to the content first and the spelling and punctuation later. They aren't always aware of all the options right at the outset, and I understand this. I don't expect them to know, or to be able to articulate, all of what they want right up front. And, of course, it's not simply a matter of what they want in general, but what they want with regard to a particular piece. I know that I want different kinds of responses from my readers at different times. Sometimes I may want a piece proofread and nothing more. At other times I want attention paid to a particular section. I know that I can, to a large degree, decide how to use the help that teachers and readers offer me. I want my apprentices to feel that they have the same ability.

Yet, as is the case with so many aspects of this work, I am always surprised by the extent to which the kids know this already and teach me by example. When they go for extended periods without sending me any work and then suddenly (or so it appears at this end) choose to make use of me again, they remind me that it's OK to use teachers sporadically, or at any rate to decide for oneself how often to use them. A couple of years ago, when I was meeting once a week with a poet to discuss my work, I discovered that having to prepare several poems so frequently was making it difficult for me to write. I needed more space around our sessions, and I needed to be able to set the intervals myself, to let the poems determine when I was ready to hear a teacher's comments.

When I told my teacher this, she had no objection to the new arrangement, and told me to call her whenever I felt ready for a meeting. I remember feeling exhilarated to discover that I had the same freedom, in adulthood, that my young apprentices had. I too could determine how I would use my teacher.

It seems to me that we continually check with our teachers to make sure that we really do have the right to decide how to use them. Maybe I feel this only because I'm unused to having that right, but sometimes I feel the kids checking with me as well. Sometimes they explain to me that they haven't been writing for a while, or that they're working on something but aren't ready to send it to me yet, or that they want me to read something but only to comment on certain aspects of it. When I honor these requests or confirm that they don't have to show me a piece until they're ready, I am in some way reminding them that they truly can decide what to use me for.

Lest I seem more passive in this description than in fact I am, let me say that respecting a child's right to control her own work and to determine how she will involve someone else in that work is not the same as being *indifferent* to the work. I'm always eager to see what the kids are up to, what further work they've done on a piece. If they write, "I'm working on two stories about such and such," I usually reply, "I'd love to see them." It's obvious that I'm interested in their work, care about it, like to see it. I couldn't pretend otherwise, and it would be foolish and unnecessary to try. But that's not the same as implying to the kids that they are under some kind of obligation to work with me on a regular basis, or that I'll be disappointed in them if they don't revise a piece after I've spent time making suggestions about it. It would be dishonest for me to pretend that I didn't know and understand that writers often don't use suggestions they're given, or need to let a piece get to a certain point before they're ready to show it.

I am aware, though, that a child could interpret even my "I'd love to see it" to mean that I would be disappointed if she decided not to show it to me. The time I spend responding to their work could make some kids think that I would be offended if they didn't follow up on any of my suggestions. But at least there is no obligation built in to the structure of our arrangement. I don't need to have a certain amount of work from them by the end of the year. Whether or not they revise a piece of work is truly their own business (unless, of course, they are writing the piece for me as editor of *Growing Without Schooling,* which puts us in a different kind of relationship).

I said that the kids aren't always aware, at the beginning, of what options they have while working with me. Sometimes I let them know. I tell them about the various ways I am willing to handle spelling, for example: I can tell them which words they've misspelled; I can tell them this *and* give them the correct spellings; or I can do nothing about spelling until they ask me to. Once they know that they do have these options, they can decide which one they prefer. I also let the kids know that I am willing to do more than just read and comment on their work; I tell them that they can ask questions about my own work, that I can show them drafts of adults' writing if they are interested. Often I respond to particular things they've written by suggesting other writers they might read or by sending them copies of other people's writing. My offers are frequently explicit and actively made, but the kids are free to refuse them.

Letting children decide when to use a teacher and when not to is more than a matter of courtesy; it is also better for their work. Because it's up to them to decide when a piece is ready to receive criticism, they have to learn *how* to decide this. What exactly does "ready" mean in this context? At what point do you trust someone else? When would comments be useful, and when would they be overwhelming? We learn this from the experience of showing our work to someone else, getting comments, and then seeing how that feels. *Was* it useful? Or was the piece too rough, our sense of its direction too unclear, for us to gain much from a critical response? Like so many other things this varies from time to time and piece to piece. With one piece we may want a reader's response at an earlier point than we would want it with another piece. And we may trust different readers at different times: I have one or two people to whom I show my earliest drafts, a couple more to whom I show the next round, and so on.

It's important to remember that adults are receptive to different kinds of help or responses at different times because we may be inclined to think that receptivity to help is a developmental matter only. We know, for example, that when children are young they are generally less interested in information about spelling and punctuation than they will be later on. This makes sense, because it's hard to take in everything all at once, and many young children invent their own spellings while focusing on getting their meaning across. But let's not forget that when children don't want us to tell them which words they misspelled or which punctuation might be more appropriate, it isn't *just* because they aren't developmentally ready to hear such things. Writers, of any age, sometimes want this kind of response to their work and sometimes do not. Homeschooling parent Nancy Wallace wrote in *Growing Without Schooling*:

> By the time she was 6, [Vita] had given me a clear understanding of how she expected me to respond to her writing. When she wrote for herself (in her journal), our family, or other close friends and relatives, she wanted no help and no sly comments about the fact that she paid no attention whatsoever to spelling and punctuation. She trusted us to decipher her messages, and when we didn't, she figured that it was simply our loss. When she wrote to people less intimate, though, she expected me to correct even the smallest error. . . . What she hated most was having some stranger call her invented spelling "cute," and she trusted me to protect her from that.[5]

Nancy is not describing separate developmental stages here: Vita wanted different kinds of help under different circumstances. Sometimes she wanted her mother to read her work only for its meaning, and would have been hurt if Nancy had interrupted with information about spelling and punctuation. But at other times she very much wanted that information, and asked for it explicitly. This isn't very different from the way adults behave. If an adult wrote a love letter and the reader began correcting its spelling, the writer would be offended. But if that same adult were writing a letter to the local newspaper, or anything else she considered public or formal, she would expect exactly that sort of response, and would ask her reader to proofread the text carefully. Adults make decisions all the time about how they want their readers to respond, and while this may sometimes have to do with what they are developmentally ready to take in, that isn't all there is to it. Nancy was right to adjust her responses according to what Vita was asking for, both because doing so was more courteous and because it enabled Vita to take responsibility for her own work.

Though I'm confident that kids know themselves better than we usually give them credit for, it's true of all of us that we don't always know what we want, right at the time, well enough to be able to ask for it. One advantage of working with kids over time is that I get to know them and can sometimes guess, or help them figure out, what they are looking for. Kim, for example, once sent me a piece she'd written about a dance workshop she'd attended. When she sent it to me she wrote, "The workshop was interesting—it taught me a lot about teaching, and working with other people, and I wrote about it in my journal last night. I think I will type up what I wrote and send it to you." I couldn't be sure, but it seemed to me that Kim was sending me that part of her journal just for my interest, rather than because she wanted me to give it the close reading and critical comments that I give when she explicitly asks me to. Here's where the limitations of working through the mail enter in: because I didn't know for sure whether Kim wanted my critical comments, I decided not to risk giving them right away. Instead, I told her that it didn't *sound* as if she was asking for comments yet, but she should let me know. She responded, "I think I'd rather you waited. Until I've gotten all my thoughts together about something, it doesn't help to start working with you on it." I'd guessed right. If I hadn't, and Kim had wanted to hear from me after all, that would have been OK too. I would have then gone on to respond to the piece, and the only loss would have been a little time.

When the kids do decide to use me, the most obvious and immediate way is simply as a reader. They want to know how a piece strikes me, if I understand what they mean, if I'm interested or moved or entertained. Beyond that, they want to know what isn't clear, what might be added or changed. When they show a piece to me (or someone else) and want those kinds of responses, it means that they are open to the idea of revising it. The work is still in flux, still malleable.

It took me a little while to be sure that the kids felt this way, that when they sent me something they truly did see it as work-in-progress rather than as a finished product. When Mika first wrote to me, for example, she sent the published copy of a story that she'd written during a week-long writing class for children at the local college. Because the story was in such a polished form, I wondered if Mika was sending it as a way of introducing herself to me and showing me what she was capable of. I was a bit hesitant to comment on it as though it were an early draft, and yet Mika had explicitly asked for comments, so I went ahead and gave them. I mentioned to her, though, that I tended to give more extensive comments on drafts of writing because the writer was more open to revision at that point.

She responded, "About first drafts—though the story I sent you was typed and had previously been published in a class I took, I might revise it further (the class was a week long—not much time) and try to get it published elsewhere. Thanks for all the comments!" I was reassured that Mika understood what sending me a story involved, and wouldn't have sent it if she hadn't wanted precisely the kind of response she got.

Ariel, similarly, told me that she wouldn't want to show someone a finished draft, because then she wouldn't be as open to criticism. She makes sure to let her readers know this; when she sent me a story that she'd written for younger children, she wrote, "This is typed only to be legible. I'm still open to revision."

I don't always know whether, or how, the kids decide to use my critical suggestions. Sometimes they simply thank me for the comments without going into detail about which ones were useful or how they plan to incorporate them. Sometimes they say, "I plan to use your suggestions," but then they don't send me the revised work. Other times they may not go back to that particular piece at all, choosing instead to concentrate on writing something new. This is all OK with me, again because I understand from my own experience that sometimes we need to sit with critical suggestions for a while before responding to them, and that sometimes we choose not to respond at all, either because we disagree or because we're more interested in working on something else.

Despite all this, there are times when the kids do respond to my suggestions explicitly and allow me to see the result. Here, for example, is eleven-year-old Emma's first draft of a story beginning:

Spirits from Down Under

Louise Terry De Kemp awoke with the sound of rain outside her cellar room window. Oh drat! she thought. No football today. I wish I was somewhere else. I wish I lived underwater or under the earth.

She got out of bed and got dressed. Putting on baggy jeans, a blue turtle neck and a blue and white checked baggy sweatshirt, she added her black high-cut Reeboks and white socks. Soft feet padded down the hall. "Louie. Mum said to call you." It was Ian, Louise's 3 year old brother. He was wearing his flannel shirt and blue osh-kosh overalls.

"Okay, tell Mom I'll be down in five minutes."

"Okay!" and Ian padded back upstairs to the hall.

Five minutes later, Ian and Louise and their mum were downstairs. Dad was upstairs.

"Sweetie," said Louise's mother. "Tomorrow is your birthday."

"I know," said Louise. All of a sudden there was a sound of an explosion. Then an "Oh Damn" from mom. The room was dark.

Suddenly Lou felt herself being thrown through mid-air. Bang!

A small noise was coming from next to her. Whimpering! Lou could see a small shape next to her in the dim light. Ian!

"Ian?" asked Lou. He gasped. "No," said a shaky voice. "It's Lou," said Lou. He let out a sigh. "OH! Lou!" He jumped into Lou's arms. They hugged each other then Ian said, "Lou, where are we? Where's mum?"

"Don't know sweets," said Lou. "Don't know."

Then: "Do you have on any shoes?"

"Yes," said Ian. "Good," said Lou.

Ten minutes later Ian and Lou were standing in a small dirt cell. Lou checked out Ian to make sure he was all right.

"A few small scrapes, but nothing much," said Lou. "Now, let's see about getting out of here." She felt around her, following the line of the old dirt wall. "Nothing!" said Lou. "Whoever caught us through the roof. Let's just try to sleep."

A small sigh, then: "Okay."

Here the story stopped, though Emma said she planned to continue it. There were all sorts of things I liked about this draft: its definite voice, the fact that Emma seemed to know exactly where she was going with it, its pace, which held my attention all the way through. Up to this point I had seen Emma concentrate on dialogue, and I was impressed by how skilled she was at writing descriptive passages as well.

There were a few parts of the story that were unclear to me. In a note in the margin, I asked Emma whether Ian was the shaky voice who said "No" in paragraph 10. I wasn't sure why he would say no—was he afraid to tell the truth? When Emma sent me the next draft of the story, she had revised the paragraph as follows:

> "Ian?" asked Lou. "Yes. I am Ian. Who're you?" he said bravely. "It's Lou," said Lou. "OH! Lou!" He jumped into Lou's arms . . .

Further on in the story, I thought that the sentence "Ten minutes later Ian and Lou were standing in a small dirt cell" implied that they had been passively carried there, but Lou's question about shoes had made me think that she was about to lead Ian on a walk through wherever they were. I told Emma that I thought she needed to make it clear that Ian and Lou had walked to the cell, as opposed to being carried there. But I had misunderstood. When Emma revised the paragraph she clarified it this way: "Ten minutes later Ian and Lou discovered they were standing in a small dirt cell." I'd been wrong; it wasn't that they'd moved to the cell but that they discovered they'd been there all along. Here was a situation in which my confusion let Emma see what she needed to do to convey her meaning accurately, even if my original guess about her meaning had been wrong.

Next, I wasn't sure what Emma meant by the sentence "Whoever caught us through the roof." I asked her, "Is it a question, or is she saying, 'The person who caught us must have caught us through the roof'? How do they know that someone caught them at all?" Emma's revision of the sentence read: "How we got here must have been through the roof." Again, my confusion apparently guided her to her own revision. Emma was able to use my responses—even my expressions of confusion—to see how one reader understood her story, and, in some cases, to clarify her own intent.

I note in passing that Emma, now fifteen, has in the past couple of years become a serious actress and spends most of her time involved with community theatre groups in her small town outside of Boston. She doesn't think of herself primarily as a writer, and yet I learned enough from our work together to make me want to include a sample of it here. Though I haven't yet been able to explore this idea much further, my work with Emma suggests to me that getting serious criticism from a practicing writer can be useful even to those young people for whom writing is *not* a central activity. It can help them with specific pieces of writing that they may be working on, and can help them feel comfortable and competent as writers in general. Though I am generally most interested in how people do the work to which they are most committed, it seems important, also, to think about how we can all remain reasonably competent at and interested in the activities we *don't* put at the center of our lives, instead of dismissing ourselves as people who "don't write" or "can't do math," or whatever it may be. Emma, though now intent on making acting her life's work, continues to keep a journal, to write occasional articles, and to exchange work with Kim through the mail. (I introduced the two of them when Kim was visiting Boston.)

I said that Emma used my responses to her story to clarify her original meaning. Something similar happened when Heidi sent me her seven-chapters-long story, "Army Life." The first draft (or rather, the first draft she sent me—it was Heidi's seventh or eighth draft) had a passage in which the main characters are told that they will have to leave the army, and then, moments later, are informed that this was a mistake. The original passage read:

> "Boys," the General began, coming up to them. "I've got bad news for you. You are out of a job. I know you would really like to stay, but President Taft said that no men younger than 18 can work on or at the army. You can pick up your checks in tent 21." With that the General turned and left.

There is some discussion about this among the characters, and then:

> "Boys! Boys! Good news!" A four-star General named Benny said, bursting into the tent. "The General just re-read the note, and he said that he misunderstood it! You don't have to go."

I found it a bit hard to believe that the General could have so completely misunderstood the note. I wrote to Heidi, "I think I'd find this less confusing if I knew what the misunderstanding was. What did the note say? It seems improbable to have the General think the note said men under 18 must leave, and then have it turn out that it didn't say that at all—unless it turns out that it said something close to that, something that could easily be confused with that."

Heidi responded to my question by having a lieutenant, rather than the General, be the one to come in with the original bad news, and then by revising the later paragraph so that the General himself delivers the following explanation:

"Boys! Don't pack. That man that just came in here was lying. There was no such note from the President. I did get a letter that said most of you will be graduating. Now, on your posts," the General commanded.

"If you don't mind sir, um, but how did that man get the idea to tell us to go?" Loyd asked as the General headed out the door.

"I think it was because I got a serious looking letter today. It had 'spy's tent' written on it. He might have just made a mistake."

Heidi apparently took my confusion seriously enough to decide that if I thought the original version was improbable, so might other readers. In her next draft she gave the explanation I had said would be helpful—about how such a misunderstanding could have happened—in a way that made the story much more believable to me.

Another example. I had a question about Ariel's story written for young children, "Miss Molly of 49th Street":

Miss Molly of 49th Street is a most peculiar person. No one knows her last name, though her landlord believes it is Magpie. No one knows how old she is. Her hair is a pale, pale blonde, or is it white? No one knows.

Miss Molly of 49th Street does all her shopping on Wednesday, and she always carries a large tote bag with her. In the tote bag there is a large onion, a metal letter opener, a pair of knitting needles, and some underwater goggles. She is a most peculiar person.

Now last Wednesday, Miss Molly of 49th Street went about her shopping as usual, but just as she was about to pick up a hybrid turnip, two men, their faces masked with long, long beards, grabbed her and stuffed her into their automobile. They roared away, kaput-put-putting into the distance.

When they arrived at their destination, a ramshackle old hut on the edge of town, the two men (whose names were Joe and Harry) tied up Miss Molly of 49th Street and threw her on the floor. As the kidnappers discussed how much ransom money they should ask for, Miss Molly of 49th Street slipped off her ropes, put on her underwater goggles, took out her metal letter opener, and sliced the onion straight through the middle.

A pungent, onion-y smell filled the room. It was enough to make a fish cry. Joe and Harry began to sniff, then they began to sniffle, and finally they burst into tears. Miss Molly of 49th Street quite calmly got out her knitting needles and knitted Joe's and Harry's beards together. Then she went home, and after a hot cup of carrot-cider tea (I told you she was peculiar), she called the police.

In the end, it took the entire police force—*with* help from the local firefighters—to arrest Joe and Harry, because the onion had smelled up the whole shack. No one could go in without crying. Eventually Joe and Harry were placed in custody, their beards unraveled, the shack fumigated, and Miss Molly of 49th Street had everyone over for onion soup in honor of the day's events.

The next day the town was still a little misty-eyed, but other than that everything was back to normal, including Miss Molly of 49th Street, who is *most* peculiar.

I loved how perfectly crafted this story was; everything fit together and yet was wonderfully surprising at the same time. My only question concerned the kidnappers' plan to ask for ransom. "Kidnapping usually implies that there's a wealthy family behind the victim," I wrote to Ariel. "How does that work in Miss Molly's case? Do the kidnappers mistakenly think there's someone who would pay? Or were they planning to ask the townspeople? This detail may not matter much to you, but perhaps you could avoid the possibility of the question coming up in other readers' minds by having them simply plan to rob her, or you could introduce additional details so that it is clear who would be paying the ransom money. What do you think?"

Ariel's immediate response was to say, "You got me on the ransom issue. I might put in some Joe-Harry dialogue to explain that they think she has money." Ultimately, when Ariel revised the story, this was exactly how she took care of the confusion. After the kidnappers tie up Miss Molly, they have this conversation:

> "Harry, is this going to work?" asked Joe, turning his back on Miss Molly.
> "Of course it will, Joe," said Harry. "She must be rich."
> "Why, Harry?"
> "Because, Joe."
> "Okay, Harry."

The kidnappers may be a bit deluded about Miss Molly's wealth, but now Ariel's readers will know why they expected to get a ransom payment for their efforts.

One of the hardest tasks any writer has is deciding how much an audience needs to be told. Sometimes this can be especially hard for young children, who may refer to "Mary" in a story without realizing that readers outside of their immediate family won't know that Mary is the writer's aunt. A reader can help by asking questions that let the writer see what she needs to add or explain: "Is Mary someone in your family?" and so on. These questions have to be genuine, of course. I will only ask them if something truly isn't clear, or perhaps is clear to me because I know the writer but won't be clear to a broader audience.

When Amanda was almost eleven, she spent three months working on a flyer that she planned to hand out to people at homeschooling conferences. The flyer was a series of questions that people frequently asked Amanda about homeschooling, or that she thought they might ask, and her answers. (Amanda, like most homeschoolers, often gets asked questions about her life and her education, and the idea of explaining herself once and for all intrigued her, as it had intrigued Kim when she thought of writing her education journal. One's answers to such questions change over time, of course, and in addition to being a good summary of home-schooling, Amanda's flyer ended up creating a vivid picture of her life *at the time*. No doubt if she were to revise it now, at almost fifteen, it would be a different piece of work.)

Most of my help with this project involved telling Amanda when I thought she needed to give her readers more information, or, sometimes, when I thought she was struggling to explain some-thing that her readers were likely to understand as it was. Here's a simple example. One of the questions on the flyer was, "What's the best encounter you've ever had with somebody who's questioned you about homeschooling?" The first draft of Amanda's answer read:

> The best encounter I've ever had was when my little sister was taking a gymnastics class and I was asked by one of the teachers what school I went to. After I had told her I was a homeschooler she said, "Oh, that's wonderful, I heard about homeschooling in college but I always wanted to meet one of you and now I have!" The *worst* encounter I've ever had was at a gymnastics class where every week a kid would ask me— the same kid, every time—"What school do you go to?" And every time, I'd tell her about my homeschooling, and every time, she'd say, "I don't believe you." That really hurt me, to think that she thought that I was sad enough about my life to be lying.

It wasn't clear, from the wording of this draft, whether both encounters had taken place in the same gymnastics class, or whether Amanda was referring to two different classes. I told her that I thought this ought to be clarified. In the next draft, she changed the latter sentence to read, "The worst encounter I've ever had was at a summer gymnastics camp. . . . " This is a simple revision, but it cleared up the confusion, and this is just the sort of thing we often have trouble noticing for ourselves.

Sometimes, my confusion about a line or passage doesn't inspire the writer to revise it but instead makes her want to explain why she chose it in the first place. For example, I had some questions about the first stanza of thirteen-year-old Tabitha's poem, "A Maiden's Song":

> Into this life we have come
> and women we shall be.
> On this day and on this night
> we enter in on a sweet flight
> that bears us mystery.

I wasn't sure what "this" in the third line referred to. It seemed to refer to the day of birth, but the first line of the stanza put the story in the past tense "Into this life we *have come*" so I imagined that the speaker of the poem was someone older, looking back on the coming-into-life. But then the following lines seemed to suggest that the speaker was talking in the present tense about being born.

When I wrote all this to Tabitha, she responded, "I have decided not to change anything in my poem as all of it is necessary to me; instead I will explain it to you. . . . I do not know if you are familiar with blessingways. They are from the American Indian, a kind of celebration. I was given (by my mother) a coming of age blessingway. This might help to make the first stanza clear to you. We had already been born as humans and, 'on this day and on this night' we are born as women."

Tabitha's explanation did clarify that stanza for me, and it raises the question, how important is it to work such explanations into the poem itself? It's not an easy question for any writer. Tabitha might have decided that she didn't want to risk other readers being as uncertain as I was. But she also had the option of deciding, as in the end she did, that the poem was really meant for a particular friend who had the necessary background knowledge to read it as Tabitha meant it to be read. "Clear" and "right" are not objective terms; they depend in large measure on one's intended audience.

I often find myself in Tabitha's situation. Sometimes the poets in my workshop will be confused about something I've written, but will then say, after I've explained it a bit further, "Oh, I see now; never mind, it's fine the way it is." But is it fine? If they needed the explanation to understand the poem, shouldn't the explanation be imbedded within the poem somehow? Or is it merely that after one or two more readings, the poem itself became clear? What if one person in the workshop is confused and the others are not? How much should the one confused reader influence whether or not I revise the poem?

This is why the poet who leads the workshop constantly urges us to get another opinion, and why I am careful, when I respond to kids' work, to say, "I'm just one reader; you'll have to decide how much weight to give to my responses." Kids who have already had several readers are probably more familiar with this. Before we began working together Heidi had already shown "Army Life" to her mother and to her teacher in school (Heidi went to school before becoming a homeschooler). I asked her whether she had found her mother's and her teacher's responses helpful, and she replied, "I appreciated Mr. M—'s opinion, but I didn't necessarily take everything he said. He wanted the story longer, and more conversation, and Mom wanted more description and less talk. I realized that I would really have to put what I liked best in, which is a little more conversation than description. What do you think?"

Making sense of readers' diverse opinions isn't easy for anyone, and maybe it would be simpler if there were right and wrong answers that we had no choice but to accommodate. Yet I think that the process of learning to use readers is a fascinating one, and I like to watch young writers gain confidence in their ability to judge their own work and maintain a receptivity to others' opinions at the same time.

It's true, too, that in the process of defending or explaining a line we often discover more about our original intentions than we had known before. Sometimes we find out what we meant in a particular poem or story by looking at it through the eyes of a reader. A simple question from me about Chelsea's poem, "The Wish of a War Horse," led her to reflect on the poem more fully.

The Wish of a War Horse

Oh, for the love of a demon god!
To see, just once, the lowering of an aquiline nose
or, at last, a supine brow devoid of arrogance.
Cruel, shifting eyes, if only they would stop
their restless crossing and clutch the steadiness of mine!

Oh, for the touch of one iron gloved hand!
To stroke the inner recesses of my ears
and shred the sluggish lining of my heart.
Two flat, rough palms, could they rest, passionless
on the long plane of my back and the tassles of my mane?

And oh, those restless, tyrannical footfalls!
To hear them turn, spiked soled boots grating on marble,
and walk, then run ahead of the amethystine cape
    that flies like a boy's.
Running to my stable, down my corridor, to my stall
and feeling him sobbing, pressing his face against my neck
and twisting my brindled skin until I neigh with love.

In the midst of commenting on other aspects of the poem, I asked Chelsea why she had used the word "passionless" in the ninth line. She responded:

Well, I thought that the demon-god would be full of blood lust, thoughts of battle, mercylessness. So the horse would like it if his master would be calm and quiet for once. I think that's also why the horse wants him sobbing in the end. The horse wants, I think, to finally see his master as a human and not a powerful, cruel war leader. He wants to see him as he is inside, rather childish, afraid. And the horse wants to be the only one whom the master will reveal his true feelings with. That is the Wish of a War Horse.

The way Chelsea says, "I think that's why the horse . . . " and "The horse wants, I think . . . " suggests that she feels the poem coming *through* her, to some degree, so that even she can learn from it as she reads it again, can further speculate about its meaning. It reminds me of the time that my four-year-old friend Andrea, while dictating a story into a tape recorder, suddenly stopped in midstream and exclaimed, "This is an interesting story!" as though the story were being given to her or being told through her, and she, as much as her listeners, was marveling at it.

When Kim was fourteen she visited my office for a week, and we had a chance to work together in person instead of only through the mail. She enjoyed helping in the office and learning about my and my colleagues' daily work, as well as the adventure of visiting a new city and being without her family for the first time. She also enjoyed the chance to hear my thoughts about her writing immediately, without having to wait for a letter to travel between us. She was working hard on her education journal during this time. Because some parts of the journal could stand independently as essays, Kim spent some time typing those sections into the office's computer and then revising them with me. With her typical interest in analyzing her own working process, she wrote in her journal one evening about the experience of working with me earlier in the day:

There was one paragraph that Susannah questioned me about—did I really mean what I was saying? (She knows me so well that she felt that particular paragraph was conflicting with other things I'd said—she was right!) So I said, no, the words I'd written did not really say what I meant them to say. So we talked a bit about what I really meant, which helped me clarify my thoughts. Suddenly I felt that I knew exactly what I was trying to say, and how to say it, so I began typing, and turned my thoughts into words just like that, without pausing over anything. As soon as I began typing, Susannah quit talking and stepped back, knowing that I'd gotten it figured out, and just needed to be left alone to get it written. When I'd finished, I turned to Susannah and said, "OK," meaning, "Come and take a look." She did, and said, "Great. That's good." And that was it—no further revisions, nothing! It was so neat; I'd never done anything like it before—just turned around and revised something, not stopping to think over a certain word, etc. . . . I think it had to do with Susannah being there to talk to, and bounce ideas off of, to give responses which stimulate more thought.

As Kim's passage shows, interaction with a teacher can act as a mirror: it can let us see our own work and intentions more clearly. The better we get at using teachers, the more specific we can be about what we want them to tell us or help us see. Instead of just saying, "What do you think of this?" we learn to say, "Does this line fit in with the rest of the piece? Do I repeat this phrase too much?" and so on.

Amanda, sending me the second draft of a story, wrote specific questions in the margins about spelling and punctuation—whether the period should be inside or outside the quotation marks, for example. When she sent the third draft, she said, "I'd especially like your opinion on the newest part." Amanda's specific questions let me know what she was concentrating on during each draft, so that I could focus my comments accordingly.

Chelsea asked an equally specific question about a poem she sent me. In her accompanying letter she wrote, "I'm a little worried about one of the poems enclosed, 'The Wild Hunt.' I don't know about the switch from describing Herne and his hounds and their actions in the 4th stanza to describing the farmers and *their* actions in the 5th and 6th stanzas. Am I being clear?"

When the question is about clarity, the best way to get an answer *is* to ask someone else, or lots of other people. But when there's a way for the writer to answer her own question, I try to let her know about it, so that she'll know that relying on me isn't her only option. I told Amanda that she could answer many of her typographical questions by going to books on her shelf and looking at how they used punctuation in dialogue, and so on. I don't mean that doing it that way is better than asking me the question, but I wanted Amanda to know that she had the tools to answer her own questions if she ever needed or wanted to.

When teachers are active readers, rather than merely graders or evaluators, we can learn from them that writing never ends. I know that readers' comments make my work better. I have come to need and expect such comments and to leave time for getting and responding to them even when meeting a tight deadline. But whereas the grades I received on school papers signified an end, comments from readers remind me that writing never really ends. A grade is a final pronouncement; useful comments are an invitation to go further, to continue—provided, of course, that one's relationship to one's work is such that one can imagine revising it in response to others' comments. Even when my friends and I did receive comments on our school papers, we saw their purpose as justifying the grade rather than encouraging us to continue with the writing. I think it's safe to say that it's a rare student who revises a paper that has received a poor grade—or, for that matter, one that had received a good grade—unless such revision is required or actively encouraged in the particular classroom. The assignment-and-grading system encourages students to see their work as finished when it's handed in. But, again, outside of that system I am constantly reminded that writing doesn't end. Publishing a piece is, of course, an end of sorts, but even then people sometimes respond and I work those thoughts into another piece or adapt the original work into something longer. It goes on.

Teachers, or active readers, can be useful to young writers in many ways. But although this is true, we wouldn't be doing young writers a service if we told them it was true before they had a chance to figure it out for themselves. As is so often the case, it's the figuring out for oneself that's important. Kim showed me this when she wrote the following passage in a letter to me, after we'd been working together for about a year:

> I used to feel that I had to work and work on a piece and perfect it as best I could before I sent it to you, so you wouldn't have to make many suggestions for changes or revisions, because I found it hard to get used to someone criticizing my work, and so I felt that if I made it perfect enough it wouldn't have to be revised. I felt that having someone else suggest changes, revisions, etc. made the work less original, less mine. Now I realize that having someone do this offers

me *more* possibilities and freedom than ever could have been available if I did not have a teacher.

. . . I think there was a time when I was focusing more on what you would think of what I'd written than really working on saying what I meant or what I wanted to say. Now I revise and am critical of my own work as I used to be, but it's very hard to be your own most critical critic! You are very sharp, and don't miss anything, so I can count on you to show me all the things I missed —this could make me lazy, but I'll be careful. You really keep me on my toes—I have to be ready to give account for and explain my thoughts and ideas for everything I write. I work harder to make sure I'm saying exactly what I mean, that I'm to the point and don't wander. . . . Before, I looked at making revisions and changes as something that needed to be done before whatever I'd written was "finished," but now I *enjoy* the process of it, as much as I enjoy the first draft.

Kim gives a wonderful answer to the question "Why would anyone choose to work with a teacher if she didn't have to?" She has learned how a teacher can help her do what she wants to do, and do it better. But she had to learn this *from* our work together. I couldn't have told her, at the outset, that she would benefit in these particular ways. Many writers far older than Kim have trouble accepting criticism from others or subjecting their vulnerable early drafts to outside scrutiny. It took Kim less time than it takes many people to learn that critical readers can be helpful. I think Kim's sense of writing as her own work, rather than anyone else's, is largely responsible for this. Getting better at writing was *her* goal, so she was quick to recognize something that would help her reach that goal, even if it was unfamiliar. Something made her want to work with me in the first place, and something made her continue even when she found it hard to adjust to. Like the kids I described in chapter 1 who preferred useful criticism to empty praise, Kim's interest in becoming a better writer made her recognize and learn to work with whatever she found that would help. Her way of describing what it means to write better is important here, too: it has to do with becoming more effective at saying what *she* means, what *she* wants to say, not with meeting my standards or getting my approval.

There is probably something about being able to decide when to use teachers, in and of itself, that ensures that kids won't do it until they're ready to. I think that Kim was more ready than not, even at the beginning, or she would not have responded to my offer at all. When a young writer has never worked with anyone before, or even, in some cases, shown writing to anyone, and then decides to respond to my offer of help, she must know, somehow, that she is ready to make use of that help. As I've described, the kids generally had some idea, even early on, of what they wanted and why a teacher would be helpful, but a good portion of that knowledge could only become apparent to them during the course of our work.

THREE

The Writing Culture

When I told my friend Katherine, a poet, the story about my reading the *Writers at Work* series, she wrote:

> The wonderful thing about that *Writers at Work* series is how it makes you realize there is no single "right" way to write. One novelist makes elaborate outlines; another jots notes on 3 x 5 cards and keeps them in a shoebox; another can't do a thing without the first and/or last sentence clearly in mind; another writes chapters at random, pins them to the wall, and then figures out how to weave them all together. In other words, whatever works is the right way to work. I'm fascinated by poets I know (including my son Nathaniel) who can work and rework almost entirely in their heads. I have to write *everything* down, and my worksheets would fill the Grand Canyon. But what really matters, in the long run, is the poem itself, and not what mechanisms we used to get it out there.

I agree with Katherine that one of the most fascinating things about writing is the many ways people do it. As I've said, part of what interests me about the young people I work with is that they are not told how to work (or what to work on, or when to work on it). They discover how they work best by trial and error, or simply by doing what makes sense to them. Ariel told me that she usually has the first draft of a story written in her head before she even sits down to put pen to paper. Heidi, on the other hand, told me that her long fictional work about army life has gone through seven or eight drafts. Ariel was able to figure out that she prefers to do a good part of the work in her head because no one tells her when it is time to write down a story or requires that she put it through any more drafts than she considers necessary. She may know that some writers write everything out (as Katherine does), just as Heidi may know that some writers do a great deal of work in their heads, but knowing those things doesn't make Ariel or Heidi worry that their own methods of working are wrong.

The more I learn about how young writers work, the more I wonder how it would ever be possible to establish a writing program that would suit everyone. Mika, now twelve, says that she works better if she writes every day. "It's hard to get back to stories after a week of not writing," she told me. "You forget what your ideas were, and sometimes if you don't write for a while you forget how much fun writing is." But Kim, now fifteen, has learned that she needs to take time off from writing now and then. She would certainly balk at any program that required daily writing—or, at least, that required daily writing of a particular piece. Mika's writing, on the other hand, would probably suffer if she were in a classroom or program that did not make time for writing every day. (I suspect, though, that even Mika would not have thrived on a daily writing routine if she had been subjected to it before she had time to discover its value for herself. She learned that daily writing was important to her from the experience of *not* doing it and not liking the consequences. Only now that she has made that discovery is the self-imposed regimen meaningful and useful to her.)

Working independently gives these young writers the chance to discover their own ways of working without having to feel that their individual approaches deviate from some norm. But appreciation of variety among individuals isn't all they end up with, or all they want. As a matter of course they also seek out the sum of those parts, the broader community of writers.

Though I agree with Katherine about what the *Writers at Work* series can show us, the books were especially important to me, as a teenager, because they gave me access to that broader community. In addition to showing me the diversity in the writing experience, they gave me the feeling that there was something common, or shared, about that experience. Writing was my way of responding to and making sense of what happened to me, and I wanted to know and hear about other people for whom the same was true. I was hungry for the feeling of being part of a community of people who loved what I loved and did what I did. Just as David Deutsch talks about offering young people a chance to "participate in the physics culture"—to see how physicists think about the world, approach problems, talk about their work; to discover what constitutes physics as an activity and physicists as a community—so did I want a chance to participate in the writing culture.

Talk about writing can become confusing because we sometimes mean the literal act of transcription and at other times mean storytelling or poem-making or in other ways saying things for the record. We say that Ariel was *writing* in her head as opposed to simply *thinking* in her head because she was making something, planning to set it down in an organized way, shaping, rearranging, and so on. At still other times we mean something even broader, as I did when I said that writing was my way of responding to things that happened. It may be useful here to differentiate between literacy and writing. More people are literate than consider themselves to be writers in the sense of being people who write stories, poems, and so on. Frank Smith speaks of children "joining the literacy club"— that is, becoming people who read, put words on paper, etc., and learning all the conventions inherent in those acts. He calls it a club because of the communal or cultural components of becoming literate. A child learning to form words on paper learns the particular ways in which they are formed, in which direction they are written (in his or her language), and all the other conventions of transcription, and learns those things *so as to* participate in the community of literate people, to say something that can be understood by others.

When I talk about the writing culture I am essentially referring to a subset of the literacy club. The young people I work with are already fairly comfortable with the conventions of transcription; they have joined the literacy club. I am interested now in how they become curious about and gradually join the writing culture, after having developed a strong interest in writing on their own.

Often these young people, while working independently, discover something about how they themselves work that turns out to be common knowledge, or common experience, among writers. Chelsea, at thirteen, made an observation about the first draft of a story she had sent me some weeks before: "It was the first copy and when I start writing, my pen can't keep up with my thoughts and I completely forget about spelling." Chelsea told me this as though it might have been a peculiarity of her own style, but in fact many writers have the same experience of first getting their thoughts down and later attending to typographical details.

Others of the kids have at various times discovered or observed that it can help to put a difficult piece of writing aside for a while, that ideas not written down are often lost, that sometimes it's difficult to judge, by yourself, whether your own work is clear. Again, these are all common observations; none seems unusual to an experienced writer. But that is the point. We discover what makes sense in our own work and then find out that it resonates with the experiences or assumptions of the community of people doing the same work. These young people, learning about rough drafts or how to judge their work or how to handle writing blocks, are learning about these things as practicing writers rather than as students who are expected to learn them *in preparation* for one day joining the club. That's the twist: I say that these young people are learning independently and only later coming to take part in the writing culture, but that isn't wholly accurate. By learning independently and making these common discoveries they join the culture, even before they join it in other active ways. They are members of the culture of writers by virtue of being practitioners of the same craft.

This is why I find myself saying that the kids participate in the writing culture even when they are working in relatively solitary ways and seem not yet to be participating in anything at all. By participation I mean something like "working in the ways of" or "working in keeping with the conventions and practices of."

When the kids make discoveries about their own work, on their own, they have no way of knowing, at first, whether those discoveries are unique or common. But they learn what is common to the writing culture by telling me (or someone else, or by reading about it) what they have discovered and hearing the answer, "Yes, that's what writers do." In a sense, they learn that they have been participating in the writing culture all along. I, on the other hand, learn what is common to the writing culture by hearing what they have discovered on their own *before* anyone has told them that that's what writers do.

We don't *need* direct experience with other people to gain access to the writing culture or confirmation of our own experiences; as my own experience shows, we can get this from books as well. But teachers who practice what they teach (to use Frank Smith's phrase) can be very valuable in both respects. In addition to commenting on the writing they send me, I always offer to answer young people's questions about writing in general or about my own work.

When eleven-year-old Jenny first wrote to me, she asked, "Do adult writers think of a plot before they write a book, such as 'a cat that could talk' or 'an old grandpa and his adventures on the moon' and then write the book around the plot?" It's hard to give anything but a general answer to a question about adult writers in general, but in my answer I tried to give Jenny a sense of how writers could handle, or have handled, the question she raised. I told her that I thought some writers did think of ideas for characters, as she suggested, and then figure out what would happen to those characters. Others, I said, probably start writing and only then see where their character is taking them. I talked about getting ideas from things that have happened, people one has known, places that evoke a certain feeling. I talked about writing as a way of describing what one has observed about people, or what one thinks is true about the world, or how one feels about things.

When Jenny wrote the next time, she wanted to know how I get ideas for writing. She had moved from the general to the specific: if I was going to say that "some" writers did this and "others" did that, she wanted to know how I fit into that scheme.

This impulse to get to know our teachers, to hear about specific experience, seems to me quite common and sensible. After Kim and I had been working together for quite a while, she said, "I was thinking the other day that we mostly talk about my writing, and not so much about yours, and I think I'd be interested in knowing more about it, if you'd like to tell me."

These days Kim routinely asks me questions about my own work, and I don't always have ready answers. Sometimes her questions invite me to look more closely at just how it is I *do* work. Recently, for example, she wrote:

> Since I have several different writing projects going on right now, I'm trying to figure out how to handle them all. How do you write separate articles simultaneously? Do you think it's possible to work on them all at once? When I'm working on any of the articles, I'm giving it my whole concentration—I'm not thinking about any of the others—so I don't

think I'm compromising the quality of the articles. In some ways it's better to have more than one project going at a time, because if I get stuck on one article, I can work on one of the others, so I'm still writing.

I had to think about and discover my answers to Kim's questions as I wrote my reply:

> I think I usually do work on one thing at a time, basically. That is, I tend to have one project dominating my consciousness at one time, one project that my mind reaches for and plays with when I'm walking down the street, falling asleep, etc. That doesn't mean I'm not writing anything else at the same time, because I do have other writing that I have to do in the ordinary course of work at the office: letters, and some of the more routine parts of the magazine. But I do see your point about having somewhere else to go, so to speak, when one article gets difficult. I *think* that for me the size of the project determines the extent to which I can easily turn my attention to something else. If I were writing a short article and took a break from it to let a friend read it and give me comments, I might turn my attention to something else while I was waiting. But when friends were reading drafts of [this book], I didn't use that time to do any major work on another project. I used it to catch up on the more regular daily work here and to let my thoughts drift idly to the book now and then, storing up ways to revise it when my friends sent the drafts back and I got back to work. When I'm working on something that big I do tend to think about it all the time.

In asking about handling several projects at once, Kim appealed to my greater experience but also spoke confidently from her own, making our relationship both pedagogical and collegial at the same time. We gain access to the writing culture through practitioners—through people who are actually writing, as opposed to people who cannot speak from experience. A fourteen-year-old writer I know told me that he had been showing his writing to someone but was dissatisfied because "she's working with me like a teacher, not like a writer." That describes precisely why I could not make my high school teachers' comments meaningful. Instead of saying, "This is what I did," or "This is how I do it," they said,

"This is what you did" or "This is how you do it." Instead of speaking from their own experience, they spoke as though they knew the nature of my experience. But I wanted to hear from experienced practitioners, not merely experienced teachers.

When the practitioners I heard from in the *Writers at Work* series talked about using methods that were different from mine, I could simply take an interest in what they described. Nothing in their way of telling it implied that their way was the only way, so it was merely interesting to hear about different paths to the same end, just as Katherine suggested. In the same way, when Jenny and Kim asked me about my own writing, and got real answers drawn from actual experience, they were given a piece of the writing culture that might confirm their own experience or might, just as easily, have seemed to them quite foreign or unusual. They might have thought, "Oh yes, I do that too," or they might have thought, "What a funny way of working; I certainly don't do that." But in neither case would they have reason to doubt the authenticity of the response to their question. In both cases, the response would help them understand and articulate their own methods more clearly.

Sometimes the kids want more than just answers to questions; sometimes they want to *see* how adult writers work. Children living with parents who write, or children who have a chance to hang around or help out in an office where writing goes on, see, as a matter of course, that writing involves revision, that writers often use readers to help them see where their words have been effective and where they need work, and so on. Working with young writers through the mail doesn't allow for this full view of the process of work, but I've managed to come up with some ways of letting the young people into adult working life nonetheless.

In the letter in which she asked how I got my ideas, Jenny also asked to "see some drafts of writing with revisions." I sent her an unpublished essay by John Holt that had his revisions pencilled in. Working in Holt's office gives me access to these rough drafts and unpublished manuscripts, and because Holt worked before word processors were common and wrote his revisions right on the early draft, his manuscripts are perfect for showing young writers what revision looks like. I wrote to Jenny:

> It might be interesting for you to look at his first and second choices of words or phrases, and see what the differences between the two are—try to guess why he made the

revision. Sometimes, I think, he made a change that would make the language itself smoother or clearer—maybe substituting one word for several, for example. Other times, I think the revision changes the meaning slightly. The main thing is that you can see that writing involves all sorts of decisions like this, many choices both little and big.

I have since sent the same manuscript, or something similar, to a couple of other kids. It seems to me very important to do this, because it's so easy for children to think that when we suggest they revise their own work we are doing it because they don't yet write perfectly, the way we do. Most of the time children see our finished products. They don't see writing when it's on ordinary paper, in our handwriting or in ordinary typescript, with typographical errors, misspellings, and so on. When we suggest revisions to children in this context, they may easily think of those suggestions as *corrections* that they, because of their inexperience, need to make. Of course, in some specific cases this may be true. My comments on a child's writing may (though not always) be full of more notes about spelling and typographical conventions than would my comments to an adult writer, simply because children are newer to those conventions. But everyone revises. The more we can convey to children that revision is simply a part of writing, the way sanding is part of carpentry or rehearsing a scene is part of acting, the better. It's not a punishment or a chore because you didn't get it right the first time; it's part of doing what writers do.

I'm often impressed by the extent to which the kids I work with have already learned this, even before I arrive on the scene. Rather than having the idea that they should be able to "get it right the first time," they seem to equate ability to revise with increased skill. Tabitha, at fourteen, said, "The better I write the more rough drafts my writing has to go through." I'm not sure whether she meant that the better she writes the better able she is to see what needs to be improved or that as time goes by her standards rise so that more revisions are necessary, but in either case it's clear that she sees ability to revise as a sign of growth rather than as a sign of defeat.

Ariel told me that she regularly goes back and revises her private diary. "How come," I asked her, "when no one's going to see it?" "*I'm* going to see it," she answered, and I marveled at what this revealed about her sense of craftsmanship. Some writers, to be sure, enjoy the freedom not to revise that private diaries grant them. But it's clear that Ariel doesn't see revision as something you do to please someone else.

Desire for the writing culture involves more than just interest in how others work. When Kim was fifteen she wrote to me, "I guess maybe I've come to the point where just doing my own writing isn't enough for me—maybe I need to be doing something with other people." The desire to take an active part in the writing culture, to join with others, seems to arise naturally as interest in and commitment to writing grows. Teachers in schools, recognizing children's desire to belong to a community of writers, sometimes set up libraries of the children's work or arrange for the class members to read and criticize each other's work, and perhaps to discuss common challenges and problems. When young writers aren't in classrooms, it isn't as immediately apparent where they will find their writing community or who will be the members. Some find it in the community of homeschoolers. More and more homeschoolers seem to be forming what they call writing clubs, which function more like the traditional adult writers' workshop than like classes. That is, people bring the work that they have been doing at home and read it to get others' reactions, as opposed to doing assignments or exercises. Gradually, the members learn to be active readers—to give specific responses instead of just general praise. When I interviewed thirteen-year-old Nathan about the writing club he belongs to, he described the process as follows:

> When you start a writing club, as in most new situations, you don't really feel comfortable with everybody else, so most of the comments are in the category of, "That was really brilliant" or "I liked that a lot." As we began to know each other more intimately, we started giving more comments about what we really felt, not just what we thought the others would like. We started being able to say, "I liked that part in the story, but I think you could do something else better in this other part." That will come when everybody really feels comfortable with everybody else.
>
> It's not really that helpful for you, as a writer, to hear, "That was great." You don't learn that much from that aside from the fact that they liked it. If they tell you something that

they didn't like, you have something to work on. . . . When people don't comment, it becomes more of a story hour than a writing club. You're just listening to other people's writing, so it's more of a reading club.

Mika, too, recognizes that having a regular audience will give her something that working alone cannot. She and a friend started a newspaper, called *Neighborhood News*, which they have been publishing regularly for the past four years and distributing to friends in their Wisconsin neighborhood. The copy that Mika sent me includes book and concert reviews, reports of the editors' activities, and a column of local news and gossip called "Route One Rumors."

When Mika and her friend saw that people were interested in what they had written, they were encouraged to continue. "If you know you have someone who wants to read what you write," Mika told me, "it helps a lot." Now, having heard about the writing clubs that homeschoolers in other parts of the country have organized, Mika thinks she might try to start her own club. She said, "I think a writing club would give me a broader audience, and would give me more incentive to write stories—I would know the club was waiting to hear them."

Meanwhile, Mika has already participated in the writing culture in two other ways: she has begun volunteering at a local newspaper, and she has spoken to a group about her work. About the first experience, she wrote:

A friend of ours, who is on my dad's softball team, is one of the editors of the *Ashland Daily Press*, which is printed fifteen miles from our house. Early in the summer Mom asked him about me volunteering there, and he said he'd be glad to help me.

First he gave me an assignment: write a review of a local hiking trail for the paper. After I had done that he asked me to come to the office and he introduced me to the staff there. Then he worked with me on the computer and I worked on typing. I also learned how to use a 35 mm camera and took some pictures. Then I got to use the darkroom there and develop them—it was really neat because I've never done anything like that before.

For my next assignment I wrote a story on apple picking (first, of course, I had to go pick some apples). It was published in a section on Apple Fest, which is held in a nearby town in October.

Writing articles for the newspaper was not much different from writing for *Neighborhood News,* the newsletter I publish, because I basically just gave it to them and they printed it with a few minor changes. I did several drafts before submitting it, of course, but it really was pretty easy and fun.

After working with our friend for a couple of months I was getting bored with it, because every time I wasn't doing something he had me type press releases, which I found out was extremely boring. I had met another reporter, Mary Thompson, who worked at the *Daily Press* too, so I decided to try and work more with her. She had suggested to me early on that she would be willing to let me go with her and do a story, so I called her and we lined up a day. I would go to a Catholic school with her—she was doing a story on a teacher there, and I could come along. I really got a taste of what you did on an interview. She suggested I write an article on Penokee Mountain Cooperative School, which is the resource center for homeschoolers that I attend, for National Education Week. I did, and it was published. This was my longest article yet and I was really excited!

I'm still working with Mary and I'll probably be doing more and more stories, which is great. Working at the newspaper has been a really fulfilling experience and I'm glad I got up the courage to try it.

Mika also wrote about the experience of speaking to a group of college students—certainly a less common way to participate in the writing culture—and it's clear from the opening paragraph that Mika sees herself as a serious writer:

I was asked by a friend of our family to speak in her English class at our local college, about my writing career. She wanted me to talk about *Neighborhood News,* a bi-monthly newsletter of writing by homeschoolers that I edit, and how I write, and writing I have published in national magazines.

At first I was really nervous about it and considered turning down the offer. But then I came up with a solution. I made a few phone calls and it was worked out: my friend Nica and I would speak in front of the class. Nica is a homeschooler who writes a lot and co-edits *Neighborhood News* with me.

We outlined our presentation and got together materials we would need: books, magazines we were published in, and old issues of *Neighborhood News*. About two weeks later, we arrived at the college. Our friend introduced us to the class and we started. We explained that we were homeschoolers, which gives us the freedom to write what we want, when we want. We talked about *Neighborhood News* and how it gives us an audience. We showed and explained the magazines we had gotten published in. We told that we were read to and read a lot ourselves, and that it affected our writing. When we were finished we were surprised that our presentation had taken only half an hour!

Then the class asked questions for a while. A lot of the questions had to do with homeschooling, as many of them had never heard about it before.

At first I had been nervous, but then I realized it was just talking—and really, it was fun!

Sometimes, when we think about allowing children access to the writing culture, we think that all they need, or are interested in, is the culture of *children's* writing. Thus, homeschooling parents think about helping their children form workshops with other young writers. But this may not always be what they want. The more these young people feel themselves to be practicing writers, the more they feel themselves to be members of the whole writing culture, not just the kids' division of it. Chelsea told me that she was more interested in writing in general than in the writing of kids her own age. Mika said, "It's neat to read something somebody my age wrote—it makes me think that it's possible. But I also like to read adults' writing, because I just like writing in general." Her comments suggest that although the community of young writers is interesting to her for obvious reasons, she would not want to be limited to it. Kim made the same point even more vehemently when she responded, in her journal, to an article that had been published in *Growing Without Schooling:*

I'm not sure what the big deal is about hearing "other children's writing." I think it's interesting to read what other kids have written about themselves, their lives, etc., but if it's fiction we're talking about, it wouldn't make a whole lot of difference [to me] whether it was an adult or a child writing it. . . . Reading a novel just because it was written by someone under 18 or 21 would mean nothing to me—all that matters to me is whether it's a good book or not. I don't like it when "adult" things and "children" things are separated merely because they are adults or children—it only widens the already huge gap of communication between adults and children.

Kim is not interested in the writing of other young people, per se, although she *is* interested in young people who are writers. She would like to meet other young people who share her interests because that, in itself, is valuable. But that doesn't mean that she wants to read only the work of people her age, or to associate only with other young writers. When it comes to her work as a writer, she doesn't want to be limited to the culture of people her own age.

I think Ariel was saying something similar when she told me about the two writing workshops with which she's been involved. Ariel has had more direct experience with this aspect of the writing culture than most of the others; she started a kids' writing group in her Texas neighborhood and now attends monthly meetings of the local writers' guild, a group whose other members are all adults. Ariel said she enjoys being accepted in the adult writers' group and is happy to be taken seriously by the members. From what I've heard, from both Ariel and her mother, it appears that the group sees Ariel as a fellow writer, not just as a child writer. And yet Ariel admits that she sometimes feels intimidated by how much more experience everyone in the group has (several are published writers).

She would like to be part of a kids' writing workshop too, because, she says, "We'd understand what we were all going through." "In what sense?" I asked. She said she meant that other kids would understand the experience of not being taken seriously as a young writer. They would sympathize with Ariel's feelings about adults saying, "Oh, you're going to be a writer when you *grow up.*" So it's not that Ariel wants to read writing by young people, specifically; her point is that young writers share certain experiences (her emphasis was on the negative ones, but she may have others in mind as well), and it would be nice to be in a writing group where those experiences could be discussed.

Kim's and Ariel's comments made me realize that although adults often provide forums for children to publish their writing, we don't, as often, provide (or help them find) ways for them to get together and discuss their own work. There are more magazines and newspapers of children's writing than there are publications in which children can discuss their work or conferences and workshops for the same purpose. Maybe we need a *Young Writers at Work* series.

One of the things Ariel has discovered, from her experience with both writing groups, is that finding a group is not always enough. People may have different expectations of the group or may not be able to learn from each other. Finding a workshop that is truly useful is much like finding a teacher who is truly useful; the more we know about how we work and what we are looking for, the better chance we have of finding one. Ariel described an experience she had in the kids' group: she told another girl that she really liked the story she'd written but thought she was using the word "said" too much. The girl got offended and the group didn't last long after that.

"She has to learn how to accept criticism," said Ariel, who seems to have developed a remarkable ability, from an early age, to do just that. She says that in the adult writers' guild she is learning a lot about how to critique someone else's work. Will she be able to get everything she wants: a group that gives and accepts criticism in the way she wants and also understands the challenges that confront a young writer? Maybe. Her desire for participation in a community of writers is strong, and I don't think she's yet given up on finding the kind of participation she wants.

Another way of gaining an audience, and of participating in the writing culture, is publishing your work. Some of the kids have had no experience with this; others have been published in national magazines like *Stone Soup*, which publishes children's work, or local publications put out by homeschooling groups. Most have, through their association with me, had pieces about their homeschooling or related issues published in *Growing Without Schooling*.

Some people who are interested in children's writing say that children should concentrate on developing their skill at writing itself before they turn their attention to publishing. Others find it hard to imagine that children would be inspired to write unless they could anticipate the reward of seeing their work in print. In my experience, young writers are, on the one hand, *less* interested in publication than we might think and, on the other hand, are not harmed by trying their hand at it if they choose to. That is, I have found that kids will revise and otherwise work seriously on pieces of writing without any thought of publishing them. They don't need that incentive to devote energy and attention to the work. In time, though, this aspect of the writing culture becomes as intriguing as the others.

Ariel, for example, wrote in a letter to me, "I would like to start marketing my work now, instead of waiting until I'm an adult. Do you think I should wait?" I replied:

I'm certainly not going to tell you that you should wait, because I know how infuriating that can be when you want to do what's important to you right now. The only things I can say about the question are these two: first, ask yourself whether you would be able to handle having a story rejected by an editor. It's inevitable that this will happen; it happens to all writers. Some people feel that their writing or their feelings about their writing are too vulnerable to withstand this, and they decide to wait awhile. Often, this varies from story to story. That is, after working on something for a while, I may say, "OK, I feel ready to send this out now," by which I mean, I've done all the work I can do on it for now, and I feel ready to throw it out to the marketplace and see what others think. It also means that I feel enough distance from it that I'll be ready to revise it if the editor says, "We'd like to publish it, but first we'd like you to revise it in the following way." . . . I may feel [that another] piece is just not ready for any of that yet, and needs more work, or simply needs to sit around for a while, or I need to show it to more people first.

So all of these are judgments that only you can make. The second question that I would ask yourself is, "Will the time and energy that I spend on sending my stories out, which includes finding out where to send them, learning what the requirements of those magazines are, and getting the stories ready to be sent, detract in any significant way from the time and energy I need for the actual work on the writing?" . . . Every writer needs to strike a balance between work on writing—which is really the most important thing—and work on marketing that writing. If you feel yourself spending too much time on the latter, you may have to pull back a bit. Now, someone might say that you, being younger, ought to spend more of your time, relatively speaking, on the actual work of writing. I would say that you should spend time on that because, again, that's what's most important for all of us writers. But I wouldn't say that you shouldn't spend time on marketing too, if that's what you want to do. If anything, you may have more time than some adults do, so striking the balance may be easier for you. Also, and this is something important to bear in mind, working on a story with the goal of eventually sending it out can be a very good thing to do—it can motivate you to revise a story that you might otherwise have let sit. . . .

There is no simple answer to Ariel's question, but I think that by giving her a sense of the ways in which I and other writers make decisions about marketing our work, I gave her some material that she can use to make the decision for herself. When Ariel wrote to me the next time, she said, "I'm fully prepared for the first (and second and third) rejection slip. My parents were very helpful in explaining that good books get rejected."

For Chelsea, writing for publication was an interesting challenge. I had told her about the "Mother's Children" feature in a magazine about self-reliance and rural living, *The Mother Earth News*. The feature is a column in which young people write about mastering something challenging or making something on their own. Chelsea's life in Alaska is so full of such experiences that I thought she'd probably have several stories to choose from if she wanted to try submitting an article to that magazine.

After a while, Chelsea decided to write about the experience of training her Norwegian Fjord colt. I think she chose this experience because she'd already written a shorter version of the story for *Growing Without Schooling*. Her article was accepted and published in a new magazine, *Back Home*, that the editor of the *Mother Earth News* column had recently founded.

The project of expanding on and revising that story, and ultimately submitting it for publication, introduced Chelsea to the world of query letters and editorial suggestions—important and perhaps exciting aspects of the writing culture. She told me afterwards that she had never written such a long, focused piece of nonfiction before, and that it was much harder to revise the article than to revise poems or stories. "I had to decide what would be interesting to others, not just what I wanted to say," she explained.

Despite the geographical distance between us, Chelsea and I worked together fairly closely on this article. When she sent me the first draft, she asked very specific questions: "I wanted to ask you if I was going in the right direction, so to speak. I mean, is it too technical? Should I put in more facts and information about horses or more personal experiences?" Chelsea's awareness of her audience helped focus her questions about the piece and ultimately (I think) helped her do the difficult work of revising it more than once.

Another aspect of the writing culture that this experience introduced to Chelsea is the idea of writing for a particular publication as opposed to writing only for one's own satisfaction. Chelsea had to think about how the *Back Home* audience differed from the *Growing Without Schooling* audience, and how to revise her article accordingly. Kim found that the same was true when she began to write about her educational philosophy for people who were less familiar with it.

Some may wonder whether participation in the writing culture may sometimes prove too much for children. Whereas parents or adult friends may take care to say what they liked about a story before pointing out where it could be improved, an editor who rejects a story may simply reject it without explanation or reassurance. Here again, a sympathetic guide to the writing culture (as to any aspect of the adult world) can be a help to young people. If a less familiar editor asks for something or makes a suggestion that confuses one of the kids I'm working with, I can help interpret it. I can explain why parts of the professional writing world operate the way they do.

In many cases, though, young people can benefit from the kind of treatment they receive in that professional world. Two experiences, in particular, have convinced me that responding to children as an editor rather than as a parent or teacher, or giving them a chance to be in a situation in which they are writing for a magazine rather than simply to complete a teacher's assignment, can have important consequences.

Kaila, an eleven-year-old from British Columbia who later asked me to comment on a story, wrote a letter to *Growing Without Schooling* about learning the multiplication tables. I wanted to print the letter, but Kaila had left out a couple of words, and in a couple of places I was unsure what she meant. I wrote back telling her I'd like to print the letter but couldn't tell what she'd meant to say here and here, and didn't know what the missing word was here, and so

on. When she wrote again, she clarified everything I'd been unclear about and said, "I'm sorry, I guess I should have proofread my
letter before sending it."

Now, I didn't say to Kaila, "You should have proofread your
letter." All I said was that I didn't understand what she meant in a
couple of places and that I couldn't print the letter until those
things were clear. She herself concluded that it would have been
easier for both of us if she had proofread the letter first. Although
I went ahead and printed the letter after Kaila had cleared up the
confusion, and no blame was attached to her in the situation (no
poor grade, not even a reprimand; just a businesslike request for
clarification), it was obvious to her that we would both have saved
time if she had taken care of these things the first time around. It
was obvious, too, that my confusion was genuine: I truly didn't
know what those missing words were. If I had known, I would have
supplied them, and wouldn't have pretended ignorance just to
teach Kaila a lesson. Here was a real-world way to learn the value
of proofreading, in a situation that did not attempt to make that its
lesson. The lesson simply arose out of the experience of writing for
a magazine, of participating in the real-world writing culture.

Something similar happened when ten-year-old Ehren wrote me
a brief note about his efforts to save the trees. He had started a
"Save the Trees" chain letter, which read: "Write to someone in
the government who can help save the trees. Copy this letter and
send it to two or more people." I was interested in printing the story
if he could tell us something about how he got the idea for the chain
letter, how he envisioned it working, and what sorts of things he
had done to save the trees. I wrote to him saying all this, and he
replied as follows:

> I wanted to make the chain letter short so it would be
> easier to copy and use less paper. Maybe some *GWS* kids
> would like to do it. I think each person will have a different
> idea about who to write to in the government and what to say.
> I found out who to write to from our public library. Here is
> what I wrote to our Congressman: "Dear Rep. Swift, If we
> keep cutting down trees they could become extinct. I know
> that trees have a lot of uses, like paper that I am writing on
> now, and lumber, and I am sure there are more. A lot of paper
> is thrown away that could be recycled. I have seen how when

they cut down trees a lot are left to rot. I hope you will work hard to save our forests."

Wherever I have gone with my mom and dad in British Columbia, Washington, and Oregon I have seen lots of brown mountains because all the trees were cut down. I read that a third of the Amazon rain forest has been cut down. Trees make oxygen and help produce rain, and they are important for other things too. I took part in another chain letter and that's what gave me the idea for this one. Besides this chain letter, I helped plant trees along the street by my house and I look for ways to save paper and wood.

Ehren's mother included a note with this letter, in which she said that her son "is a person of very few words when it comes to writing. His reply to your queries may be the longest piece he's ever written." Again, this child was given a real-world reason to do what parents and teachers often try to get children to do. His obviously genuine interest in saving the trees and telling others about it, and my obviously genuine editorial request for more information worked together to inspire Ehren to write the longest piece he'd ever written.

Because I was working as these children's editor, instead of as their teacher, I was able to deal directly with each specific piece of writing without seeing it as part of a larger set of problems they needed to work on. I asked Ehren to tell us more about saving the trees in complete ignorance of how hard or easy it would be for him to reply. Instead of thinking, "He seldom writes long pieces, so I'd better not ask him to do this," or, conversely, "He seldom writes long pieces, but maybe this will be a clever way of getting him to do that," I simply asked him, as I would ask any other writer, to expand his story. He responded to that serious treatment and managed to do something he had never done before.

Sometimes we can be inspired, or liberated, by people who know *less* about us than our parents or regular teachers know. Again, it was what I *didn't* know about Ehren's usual capabilities that, in this case, inspired him to exceed them. The reverse is also true. In some cases, getting to know the kids better has allowed me to be more helpful to them. The point is that the reality of the writing culture can teach in all sorts of ways; children can infer, from our genuine responses, what is common, or necessary, or appropriate.

FOUR

Writing Until You Know

In chapter 1 I described the experience of listening to English teachers in school talk as though everything a writer did had been consciously planned ahead of time. Perhaps this was what made these teachers feel comfortable advising us to figure out what we wanted to say before we wrote it down. The rule seems sensible enough, and a way to guard against sloppy writing. But the trouble with it, and why it became another of the injunctions that did not fit with what I had already begun to experience in writing, is that it implies that thinking (or feeling) always goes on before writing, and that writing is merely the record or result. It suggests that writers use writing only to record or show what they know, rather than to discover it. When I read Flannery O'Connor's comment "I write because I don't know what I think until I read what I say," and V.S. Pritchett's "I write to clear my own mind, to find out what I think and feel" years later, I felt the thrill of recognition. These quotes are included in poet and essayist Donald Murray's collection of quotations from writers, *Shoptalk*. [6] Like the *Writers at Work* series, this collection is full of reflections from practicing writers, and it's a book I would have loved to have when I was younger. I would have liked hearing that not all writers know what they want to say before they say it, but instead think *by* writing, use writing to find out what they feel or think or know.

Kim, at fifteen, said it this way: "I write because I love it, of course, but also to communicate something. And when you communicate something, you want to be as clear as you can. And yet, the writing helps me clear up my thoughts, so it's like I rewrite something to make it clearer, and yet the rewriting helps me to see things *more* clearly. So then it has to be rewritten again, because now I understand things better than I did when I started!" Kim writes not only to record or display what she knows but also to clarify her thoughts, or to find out what they are. For Kim, as the quotes in Murray's collection suggest, writing *is* thinking.

But if we write to find out what we think and feel, how does the old advice "Write what you know" apply? How can we write what we know if we don't *know* what we know until we write? And should we truly limit ourselves to things we have directly experienced? Doesn't this restrict children's subject choices, since their range of experience is so much narrower?

Sometimes it's clear that a child's story is about something the writer has experienced directly, as was the case with the story about her sister's birth that Jenny wrote when she was eleven:

> "I'm too excited to sleep," Jenny said to her brother John. She knew tonight Mom was going to have her baby.
>
> "Me too," said John.
>
> "I hope Mom will wake us up as soon as possible," said Jenny.
>
> Mom had been having contractions all day. It was April 12th and the baby was due April 10th. So Jenny knew this could be it. Could this be the day she had been waiting for for six months? She sure hoped so.
>
> "Good night," said John as he turned over and snuggled under the covers.
>
> "Good night," said Jenny, but she knew she would be up for a while. She lay in bed for a long time before finally dropping off into a peaceful sleep.
>
> "Jenny and John, time to get up for the birth of your baby," Sharon, one of the midwives, called.
>
> "John," Jenny said. "Come on."
>
> They walked into the dining room where Mom was lying on the floor. Jenny and John sat on the floor and covered up with an afghan. Ed and Anne, Jenny's brother and sister, came yawning into the room.
>
> "Anne," Jenny whispered. "Come and sit by me."

It was Jenny's job to record the birth. She got the cassette player ready.

"Jenny," said Sharon, "go and wake up your little sister and brother."

"OK," said Jenny. She walked into her youngest brother and sister's room.

"Gwen and Nick, wake up, it's time for the birth."

"OK," Nick said sleepily.

Jenny picked up Gwen and carried her into the dining room. Sharon and Eileen, the other midwife, were putting down pads on the floor for the birth.

"Jenny," Gwen asked, "what are those pads for?"

"They are for the blood and water that comes out when the baby comes."

Ed went into the kitchen and got the camera. He was going to take pictures of the birth.

Mom was moaning and groaning and little Gwen was scared.

"Why is Mom doing that?" Gwen said.

"Because the contractions are really hard, Gwen," answered Anne.

Mom squatted on the floor and pushed. She was grunting as she pushed.

There was a splat on the pads. The bag of waters had broken.

Mom gave another push and out came the baby's head!

Anne squealed and Jenny was excited. One more push and out came the baby!

"Oh look," Jenny cried. "It's so cute!"

"Reach down and grab your baby," Eileen told Mom.

Mom took the baby and said to them, "It's a girl!"

Jenny and her brothers and sisters oohed and aahed about the baby.

"Now we will cut the cord," said Sharon.

Dad cut the cord and some blood came out.

"What's the baby's name?" asked Anne.

"Mary Grace," answered Mom.

Dad brought out some bubbly juice and he poured glasses of it for everyone. Then they toasted to the baby's birth.

They reluctantly went back to bed.

"I can't wait to hold her in the morning," Jenny told John as they climbed into bed.

Jenny drifted off to sleep. It had been a wonderful birth!

It was Jenny's job to record the birth in more ways than one! Why did she decide to make the narrative sound like a story, with characters referred to in the third person, when it would have been just as easy to write about the event in a letter or as a diary entry? Perhaps she wanted to make it interesting to a broader audience, or she may have thought that it would excite her brothers and sisters to see themselves as characters in a story.

Just as likely, Jenny discovered that writing in the third person paradoxically gave her the distance to look closer, to see things more clearly. "We are blinded by standing too close to a mirror," my friend Nancy said when I discussed this with her. Third-person narration—or sometimes simply making the event into a story or poem—can remove those blinders and make it easier to write about strong or difficult feelings.

Putting events into story form invites us to remember them more precisely. To make a good story, Jenny had to put in details about how things looked and sounded and how she herself had felt that she might not have thought about otherwise. So was Jenny only telling what she knew, or did writing the story bring her closer to the experience and help her *realize* what she knew, what she remembered?

The phrase "write what you know" is misleading, because we are always using writing to get closer to whatever we are writing about. We write what we want to find out about. In the end it's impossible *not* to write what we know, because we have learned about our subject through writing.

Serena, whose interest in serious criticism I discussed in chapter 1, is now working on a story set during the Civil War. In her letter to me about the story, Serena wrote, "When I began writing it I had just finished a historical fiction book about the underground railroad. I had already known quite a bit about the subject, but I'm sure I will learn more while writing, both from doing research when I need to know stuff, and also by sort of *experiencing* it first hand while I write." While some may argue that you can't write about something until after you have experienced it, Serena knows that writing is a *way* of experiencing something.

When I responded to Jenny's story about her sister's birth, I told her that I would like to know *even more* about how things looked and felt and sounded during her experience of the birth. In making that suggestion, I was in effect saying to Jenny, "Get even closer. Find out more, so that you can tell me more." In her next draft of the story, that's just what she did. After the sentence, "They walked into the dining room where Mom was lying on the floor," Jenny added, "The room was dark, lit only by a candle, its smoldering scent drifting about." Toward the end, after the sentence, "Jenny and her brothers and sisters oohed and aahed about the baby," Jenny added, "They loved watching the midwives wrap their baby sister in cotton blankets and soft pajamas. She had such tiny toes! Jenny loved Mary's soft skin and wonderful newborn baby smell." These additions give our senses so much more material to work with—candlelight, smells, textures.

Kim, earlier in this chapter, said that writing helps her see things more clearly, so she has to rewrite to accommodate that new understanding. But then how does writing ever end? How do we know when to stop? Most of us probably stop when we have learned enough for our own satisfaction and enough to let our readers into our thoughts or into the experience. We write until we have learned enough to stop—or at least until we have learned enough for now.

One way to read critically, then, is to ask, "How close has this writer come? How much has she learned about her subject?" I tend to respond enthusiastically to a piece of writing when the writer has learned a lot, when she has come close enough to let me in. Here are five lines from Chelsea's poem "The Thoughts of Midwinter":

> I remember the grinning farrier,
> mud caked in his hair,
> his lower lip flat and blue
> from holding the horseshoe nails
> in his teeth.

Chelsea's poem gave me that farrier; because of it I can see something I would not otherwise have been able to imagine. I told her that of all the images in the poem, I especially liked that one because of how close it brought me to her subject. The lines remind me, too, that we never write *only* about something in the world. Inevitably, we also write about how we see or understand it. The writing is where we and the world out there *meet*. Chelsea's

71

lines are not only about the farrier. They are just as much about how Chelsea sees the farrier; the farrier her poem gives us is *her* farrier, or what happens when Chelsea and that farrier come together.

A homeschooling family in Pennsylvania often sends me copies of their family newsletter, which they have been publishing regularly for six years. When she was five and a half, Dory, the middle child, wrote (via dictation) this short nonfiction piece in the newsletter's first issue:

Moonlight Walk

This Christmas I got a present from Daddy and it was a book. It was called *Walk When the Moon is Full* by Frances Hammerstrom. In the book a little girl and a little boy and their mother go for a walk when the moon is full, and we decided that we should do it too. We were going to the pond and it wasn't dark at all because the moon was full. We were trying to be quiet because we wanted to listen for animals but our snowpants made little squeaks. Once we got there we decided to go around the pond but Jenny didn't want to go so Daddy stayed with her. The little lake was frozen by the little bridge and when we got half way done I stepped in the water, so we went back the other way. And when we got back to the picnic table, we ate cookies and we drank cocoa, and then we went home and we went to bed, and we're going to do it again next month.

I told Dory that I loved her image of the snowpants making little squeaks while the girls were trying to be quiet. That image took me right into the scene; I could imagine it completely. How like a writer to notice such things—the sound of snowpants squeaking, the look of a farrier's lower lip! I never understand it when people talk about writing as an escape from life. Chelsea and Dory, noticing and writing about these vivid details, are so clearly coming closer to life, to experience.

It is easy to see how this is true when we are writing about something we *have* experienced. Jenny got close enough to her sister's birth, and Chelsea got close enough to the farrier, to make those things vivid and accessible to their readers. But how can we possibly get closer to experience when we are writing about something we have never experienced in the first place? Tabitha, at thirteen, worked for a long time on a story about an imagined world called Joplon. Here's a passage from the opening of the third chapter:

> A blizzard drove furiously in their faces as the small group made their way laboriously forward. Somorei led them on across a wide open plain where there was no shelter from the driving wind and blinding snow. They huddled close together from instinct only, for it offered no warmth and their eyes and mind were focused on the path.
>
> It had been a week since they had found the star message. During this time it had grown steadily colder. Before yesterday it had been cold but there had been no snow; so cold that it had been tedious work to keep their thoughts on the road ahead. Then the storm had come up and now as night crept near, each of them drew hard on courage with which to face the coming darkness.
>
> All were weary when the snow finally stopped. Each trudged on alone with his own thoughts; and with eyes focused on the feet in front of him. The going was slow, for the snow was deep.
>
> Suddenly Somorei disappeared; the others stopped short, weariness leaving their eyes and anguish entering. Kelmar's mouth flew open; the hole Somorei had left was dark and gruesome. Kelmar began to think about horrible things that might have happened to their wizard when a tall hat appeared and then a pair of hands which grabbed frantically at the snow and pulled a very red and raging wizard out of the ground.
>
> "Before you come any further, have caution. The enemy has reached his fingers farther than I anticipated. Make sure every step is firm. The chasm here is not very welcoming!"

Is Tabitha's story any less an expression of what she knows than Jenny's, just because one is about imagined events in an imagined world and the other is about actual events in a very familiar world? I think it's safe to say that Tabitha knows Joplon as well as she knows the landscape she sees every day. Through writing about it she is getting to know this imagined world well enough to give it to her readers. Of course, in some sense Tabitha has more control over Joplon than Jenny had over the story of her sister's birth, since the latter was rooted in actual experience and the former comes completely from Tabitha's imagination. For this reason, Tabitha's knowledge of Joplon may be of a different sort than Jenny's knowledge of the birth. Yet many writers of fiction speak of being told what to write by their characters or by the demands of the structure of the plot. Yes, they can technically do anything they want with their fictional landscape, changing it in ways that they can't change external reality, but on the other hand they find that the more they learn about their imagined landscape, the more it seems to exist outside themselves, known as one knows a real landscape. Conversely, writers who draw on material from real life can change it and use it in ways that make the resulting work something other than merely a direct representation of the original experience. So in many ways Tabitha's and Jenny's knowledge about their subjects is the same.

Tabitha also knows about worlds like Joplon because she reads about them. She loves J.R.R. Tolkien's *The Lord of the Rings* series and Homer's *Odyssey*, which she told me was "the most thrilling book I have ever read." Reading, perhaps especially for writers, can be as important a way of knowing as direct experience. Nancy Wallace wrote about this in her book *Child's Work:*

> When a local author of children's books advised nine-year-old Ishmael to "write about what you know," Ishmael came to me and said, "Isn't that what I have been doing? I know all about sea adventures and buried treasure and pirates from exploring the brook and rafting in the pond, and from reading *Kidnapped* and *Treasure Island*.[7]

Children (like all of us, perhaps) *know* the literature they love, so it seems perfectly reasonable to them to let that literature inform their writing. It also means that they can use their writing to learn more about a particular kind of writing, just as they sometimes use it to learn more about a particular feeling or character or event.

I learned from Amanda that a young person could use writing this way. When she was fourteen, she sent me the following story beginning:

> Brrring, Brrring. The phone rang insistently. Brrring, Brring. Ruth looked up from her studies. *Brrring!* the phone gave one last impatient ring and then stopped. Ruth won-

dered idly how long it had been ringing, then decided it didn't matter. She returned to her homework—A plus negative B plus the volume of the illustration (D) equals . . . Ruth's mind drifted off to other, pleasanter thoughts . . . her teacher Mr. Howard's face as he discovered his class half-empty due to his tendency to say "of course" when any student asked to go to the bathroom . . . her best friend Sheila's last words as they parted after getting off the school bus that afternoon ("Now, remember, Ruth, if Dave really *does* call, don't act as if you've been sitting around all evening waiting for it. And for heaven's sake, don't get all involved in a stupid math problem or English comp and forget to answer the phone!") . . . Dave's face when he said he might call that night (like a smooth, unknown mask, not at all like what she saw every day in History and Chem.) . . . She brought her thoughts back, startled, as she felt a tap on her shoulder. The fact that it was almost a smack communicated to her that it was not the first one. "Yes, Mark?" she said, rather annoyed that her younger brother had interrupted at such a moment, just when she was about to enter her favorite daydream. "Mom says to tell you we're all going out to see *Dick Tracy*—want to come?" Ruth considered for a moment in silence, then said, "Nah, I'll stay here. Thanks anyway, though," she said as Mark turned to go.

Fifty minutes and four algebra problems later, Ruth wished she had gone with the rest of the family. The algebra was really tough, and studying alone made it just that much harder. Sighing, she decided to head over to the library where at least she'd have some company. She picked up her books and was about to head out the door when all of a sudden, she remembered that Dave might call, and if she admitted to Sheila that she had headed off to the library to study, and possibly missed a call from him, her best friend's disgust would be hard to live with. She decided to call Sheila instead and invite her over to study. She picked up the phone and began to dial.

An hour later Sheila looked up from her English theme long enough to say, "I'm *so* glad you called! Now, when Dave calls, I'll be right here to lend you moral support."

"He may not call, Sheila," Ruth said, "And anyway it isn't as if it mattered so."

Though this story is typical of a certain genre, it wasn't at all typical for Amanda. She had never, to my knowledge, written this kind of classic "young adult" fiction, and furthermore didn't have direct knowledge of the school experiences that the story described. I wondered about this turn that Amanda's work seemed to be taking, and for a moment was concerned that as she got older she might be turning her attention away from the material in her own life under the mistaken impression that only the life of the typical teenager was fit for fiction.

I kept the question in the back of my mind, but decided to trust Amanda's own instincts about the value of the project. I guessed that she was getting something out of writing this story, even if I couldn't yet say what, and I didn't want to steer her in one direction or another, especially until I had a chance to see where this story was going.

I did mention in my reply that I wanted to know more about how Ruth felt about the possibility of Dave's phone call (again, I urged the writer to get even closer to her subject). When Ruth says "It's not as if it mattered so," at the end, is she just pretending not to care so that Sheila will stop making such a big deal of the whole thing, or is the prospect of the phone call truly much more important to Sheila than it is to Ruth?

Amanda's next draft of the story responded to these questions. Continuing where she had left off, she wrote:

> Inwardly she was thinking, oh, brother, does Sheila make me mad sometimes. I just don't know whether I'm *ready* for all this boy/girl stuff. Sheila certainly seems to be, though.

I wrote back with my thoughts about this second draft. Then Amanda sent along a different story, and several weeks passed. The "Ruth" story occurred to me again only as I was beginning to think about this business of writing what you know. How did Amanda feel about that advice in light of this particular story? I wondered. Did she feel that she was writing about something completely unfamiliar (the life of a typical, school-attending teenager), and if so, did she feel strange about doing that? I decided to call her on the phone and ask her straight out.

"I guess I've picked up so much over the years, being around my friends who go to school," she answered, "that it seemed pretty natural to write about someone who goes to school. Even though I haven't personally experienced some of those things, they've happened to people close to me. But also," Amanda went on, "I've had a lot of experience reading books that were written for teenagers, written the way adults think teenagers like to read, and sometimes that's good and sometimes it's not good. When I read those I generally don't read them for pleasure, I read them to see if I like the way this adult writes for teenagers, and if I were writing for people my own age would I want to use this person's style."

"In other words," I said, "you're reading those books not just as a reader but also as a fellow writer. So what was your thinking behind the 'Ruth' story?"

"Truthfully, I wondered if I could write anything that sounded better than those books I was reading. I was disappointed in what I was reading, so I was kind of just trying it out to see, can I really do this? Every time I read those books I would plan it out in my head, how I would do it differently. I wondered, is it really so much harder than it looks? Is this something I could do?"

Well, this is why it pays to *ask* a young person about the meaning or intention behind a particular piece of work, instead of just guessing from our distant adult perspectives. It had occurred to me that Amanda might be writing the story as a way of learning more about the experience of the typical teenager, but I had not guessed that she was writing it primarily to learn about the experience of *writing about* the typical teenager.

"How do you think it turned out?" I asked her. "How do you feel about the story now, in terms of your original reason for writing it?"

She answered, "It made me feel that if that's what I really decided I wanted to do, I could probably continue the story and go on in that style of writing. But truthfully I got bored with that style, because I feel like so much out there is written that way. I liked my story, I thought it was basically unique and all that, but it wasn't totally an innovative, unusual idea, like my 'Grandma and the Girl' story." Here Amanda referred to a story she had written in the form of letters between a grandmother and a young girl. "That was a much more uncommon way to write a story, and I think I felt more proud of writing a story that way than just putting out what a lot of people could pretty easily write."

I told Amanda about how I had thought that perhaps she was using the story to get closer to, or find out more about, the life of a girl like Ruth, and asked her if writing the story had helped her to get to know that perspective better.

"I got to know Ruth well," she said, "and I got to understand her situation—I guess that's what you mean. I started feeling like she was one of my friends."

So in fact, writing the story brought Amanda closer to understanding both the writers of such stories and the characters in them. But what about those people who say you should write only what you know about? "Suppose," I suggested to Amanda, "I had said, 'Amanda, you shouldn't be writing this kind of story. You should write about a homeschooler, because that's what you know best.' Would it have been wrong of me to say that?"

Once again Amanda surprised me. I thought she would say such advice was unnecessary; her own experience seemed clearly to have taught that to me. But instead she said, "I think if that was all I was writing, then it would have been good for you to mention something like that. But really, that was only one of the stories I was working on at that time."

"I guess if you had only been writing that sort of story," I said, thinking aloud, "it would have been as if you didn't think your own life was worth writing about."

"Exactly," said Amanda.

"And yet," I said, now pushing the point a bit further, "in fact you haven't yet written a story about a homeschooler, or someone whose life is very much like yours."

"I have a notebook," she answered, "that I write in when I get grumpy, or angry, or sad—or happy, too, and I feel like *that's* when I'm writing about me, and that's private. I don't like to show it to anybody."

Writers use writing in all sorts of ways. For now, Amanda uses her private notebook to write about (and understand and learn more about) her own life and uses fiction to learn more about other kinds of lives and other kinds of writing.

"People could say," Amanda went on, "you shouldn't write about kids who go to school because you've never been to school. But I read about an author who had never done the thing that was the main point of her story, and still the story was believable and didn't have inaccuracies. I remember thinking as I read that, 'Well, if adults can write about things they don't know about, maybe you really can do that.'

"It would be much harder for a child in school to write about a homeschooler, though, partly because there aren't that many homeschooling examples in writing. But I think if you were close friends with a homeschooler, the way my friends are, you could write a very good, very believable story about a homeschooler, because you would know about the feelings of somebody who was doing it so totally differently."

Since talking with Amanda, I've thought often about her surprising comment that under some circumstances I *would* have been right to suggest that she write about her own life. The situation was of course hypothetical. Amanda clearly knew how she had been using the "Ruth" story, and knew that it was only part of a much larger body of work. She was obviously comfortable with her experiment. But I remember another situation in which I had been confronted with the same question.

Years ago I held a neighborhood writing workshop on Saturdays for children, unconnected with any school but made up of kids who went to school. Each week, a ten-year-old boy wrote the same kind of fantastical adventure stories. Then, during one session, he suddenly changed course. The story he read aloud was about a small ten-year-old boy who felt intimidated by the bigger boys on the school playground. It was a vivid and exciting piece of work, and the other kids responded to it enthusiastically.

Now, there's nothing intrinsic to a story about a small boy on the playground that makes it better than a story about talking pickles or flying machines. Indeed, many readers would probably prefer the latter. What excited me at the time, however, was that this boy seemed to realize for the first time that he could use the material from his own daily life in his writing, and furthermore could use the writing to figure out how to deal with events in that daily life (in the story, the small boy discovers a way to stand up to the frightening bigger boys). This seemed like a good and exciting discovery to me, but I couldn't help wondering at the same time if my own stylistic preferences were all that were influencing my excitement.

Whatever the case, I didn't want to make a big fuss over the boy's discovery because I wanted his own realization and satisfaction to be what kept him experimenting with this new form, rather than my praise or preference for one form of writing over another. The workshop ended, and I didn't know him well enough to keep up with him and find out where the experiment led him, or if he stuck with it at all.

Thinking about the event in Amanda's terms years later, I decided that the boy's experiment *had* been a good thing, worthy of my excitement. If we assume, from his own surprise at the success of the story, that the boy hadn't until that moment realized that the material of his daily life was as suitable for his writing as the fantastical characters he conjured up, then something important had indeed happened during that session. Amanda had said that if she had thought her own life wasn't worth writing about, that *would* have been bad and would have deserved my attention. If someone discovers that he can write about his own life, that's an exciting and potentially liberating discovery.

It isn't that the immediate is better than the imagined. As I have tried to show, stories about faraway or fantastical things can be just as much about what the writer knows as stories about daily life; writers can get as close to those subjects as to any other. But the issue that Amanda raised was about whether there are some things we feel we cannot or should not write about, some things about which we feel we should not inquire further, as the poet Anne Sexton put it. If it's limiting to feel that you have to write only what you have experienced, it's just as limiting to think that your own experience, or thoughts or feelings, do not belong in poems or stories.

During a phone conversation, Chelsea surprised me by saying that she often felt she didn't have anything to write about. This struck me as odd, because it seemed from her work that she had all sorts of things to write about. When I later asked her what she had meant, she wrote, "The things a kid can write about are pretty limited, I think. I mean, if we write about things that we have not yet done or experienced, we wouldn't be able to write about them as well as if we had experienced or watched them first hand." Chelsea added that she felt herself to be waiting, to a large degree, until she had had more experience and thus more to write about.

It sounded as though Chelsea accepted as true the concern I raised at the start of this chapter, that limited experience means limited writing, and that this limitation is endemic to youth. Yet Chelsea often wrote about distant lands or imagined events, and wrote about them well. Her range of subjects was, if anything, broader than the range of many young people I'd known. The explanation she had given of why she sometimes felt limited in her writing didn't completely fit.

Thinking about Amanda's comment and the experience of the boy in the workshop, I wondered if Chelsea, instead, was dismissing as unfit for poetry or fiction all the ordinary experiences of her life. Perhaps she felt she had nothing, or not enough, to write about because she was ignoring all the material that comes from being a fourteen-year-old in a family, with thoughts and feelings about herself and the people around her and her daily life. Some young writers are *too* preoccupied with these things, but others can be misled into thinking that poetry can never be about such personal or ordinary subjects.

On a hunch I sent Chelsea some contemporary poetry, mostly written by women, to suggest the range of things that people could and did write about. I told her I thought she might have more material than she had realized, even now, even without waiting until she had amassed a greater variety of experiences.

Chelsea replied that my suggestions had been on the mark, and that she had never felt comfortable writing directly about herself. It's too early to tell what this will mean for her. Maybe she will use my suggestion to write about more personal subjects and discover that she knows more than she thinks she does. Maybe she will find that she lacks the distance from her childhood and adolescence necessary to write about them clearly. I know that I am writing now about events from those periods of my life in ways that I could not have written then. Young people may lack not experience so much as the temporal distance from experience that, paradoxically, enables us to get closer to it through writing. If this is true, then Chelsea is right, and to some extent she can do nothing but bide her time until she gets older.

But even if we need distance to be able to write in certain ways, we *can* explore our immediate life through writing, and, more important, we shouldn't be afraid to try. Perhaps the most important element in what Chelsea told me was her awareness that her writing was more limited than it needed to be. Exactly how she had been limiting herself, and exactly what she will do about that, remains for her to discover.

In the meantime, what remains for those of us who work with young writers is the understanding that "know what you want to say before you say it" and "write only what you know" are indeed limiting dogmas. The experiences of the young people I've described here suggest the alternative: everything is writable. Nothing is off limits—not the fantasy worlds you can't really claim to know directly, not the ordinary everyday world that may seem too personal or too trivial to bother with. Write what you know, and find out more about it. Write what you want to know, until you've learned enough to stop. Inquire further. Write.

FIVE

———

Experiments and Inspired Moments

When Chelsea was fourteen and had been working with me for almost two years, sending me groups of poems and an occasional story at fairly regular intervals, she sent me a poem on which she had written the words "An experiment!" The poem read:

> I know that I
> should not have
> taken your glass of wine
> and thrown it out the window
>
> But it was beautiful.
> It looked like a
> burning, crystalline watersnake
> as it hung in the air
>
> and I am not sorry.

This was indeed an experiment for Chelsea, and one that I was excited to see. Right away, I was struck by her poem's resemblance to William Carlos Williams's "This Is Just to Say," and wondered if reading that poem had been the catalyst for her experiment. Beyond this, I was interested to see Chelsea trying something so unlike her earlier work. Until now, the poems she had sent me had always rhymed and kept to a regular meter, and it sometimes seemed as if Chelsea—like so many beginning poets—was becoming a slave to what she thought a poem had to be, instead of using poems to say what she wanted to say. Often, her word choices seemed to be dictated by the need to rhyme or to fit the rhythm of the line, and while there's nothing inherently wrong with that, the danger, from my point of view, is that the young writer whose choices are dictated by those considerations may come to feel that poetry is *mainly* a technical exercise or game rather than a way of saying something about the world or about oneself.

I suspected, too, that Chelsea herself sometimes felt limited by the restrictions that the need to rhyme imposed. One of the first poems she sent me, for example, was called "Spring" and had the couplet "Wakes up the bear asleep in his den,/all hungry and grouchy for roast spruce hen." Commenting on that poem, I wrote, "I like all the images of the things the wind does—tosses manes, dances, whistles, wakes up the bear. I have a little trouble with the bear image, though, because I can't quite believe that roast spruce hen is what a bear wakes up hungry for. Is there something else you could substitute that would work just as well? Roast spruce hen, or roast anything, seems too much like something that people, not bears, eat." Chelsea replied, "I have changed the 'roast spruce hen' in 'Spring' to 'wild ptarmigan.' I hope it rhymes well enough." I wondered whether Chelsea might have chosen a different image entirely if she had not been concerned about rhyme.

I asked Chelsea whether she had ever tried writing poetry that didn't rhyme, and she said she hadn't, although she thought it might be fun to try. I didn't press the issue when she didn't try it immediately, but continued to respond to the poems she sent me.

When she sent the "experiment" poem almost two years later, it had been a long time since I had mentioned anything about rhyming or not rhyming. It didn't seem, in other words, that there had been any direct connection between my suggestion and Chelsea's experiment. I couldn't tell whether she had stored up my suggestion in her mind all those months until it was the right time to respond to it, or whether she had forgotten my suggestion and made the experiment for other reasons.

Whatever the case, it was clear that by suspending her attachment to rhyme and meter, Chelsea had been able to allow a stronger and more interesting voice to come through. When I wrote back to her, I asked if she was familiar with Williams's work and typed a couple of his short poems into my letter (including "This Is Just to Say") to show her what I'd been thinking of.

When she wrote again, she said that she had *not* seen the Williams poems before, but that she liked them very much. I later learned that she went to get his work out of the library soon afterwards. When I tell people this story and show them Chelsea's poem, some find the resemblance between it and "This Is Just to Say" so striking that they feel certain she *must* have seen Williams's poem somewhere. But she says she had not, and I have no reason to doubt her. When she read the poem in my letter, she didn't say, "Oh yes, now I realize that I have read this before." It is possible, perhaps, that she once read the poem and forgot it, or read other writers' parodies of it without being aware that that is what they were. I don't believe that this has to be true to explain Chelsea's poem, but even if it is true, Chelsea is not conscious of it, which only underscores my belief that influence is not always consciously felt or intentionally received.

Chelsea soon sent three more poems that were in the style of the wine glass poem. It seemed as if the experiment had opened up all sorts of possibilities for her, and when I wrote to comment on the three newest poems I asked her, "Can you tell me anything about what it's like for you to be writing these different sorts of poems? How do you decide where to put line breaks when you aren't rhyming?"

She responded, "To decide where to put line breaks I usually go by ear and sometimes by the way it looks. Yes, it does feel a lot different to be writing poems like these. I feel much more freedom and can say what I want to say without worrying about rhyming and things like that."

In the months since her first experiment with non-rhyming poetry, Chelsea has not gone back to writing poems that rhyme, and she recently told me that she doesn't plan to. She expects to be writing this new kind of poetry for a while. She said she likes "being able to say things instead of just having to find words that rhyme." At first, she said, she found it hard to judge the quality of these experimental poems, because in the past she had judged by whether she had been able to find a rhyming word that fit her meaning. But now she's gotten used to it, she told me, and can judge these poems as well as any writer can judge her own work.

I asked Chelsea if she knew what had made her try the initial experiment, and she said that it was reading Kenneth Koch's book about teaching poetry, *Rose, Where Did You Get That Red?* The book has many examples of non-rhyming poetry (both classic and student-written), and after reading some of it Chelsea decided to try it herself.

It's tempting to think that what worked for Chelsea would work for others just as well. If Kenneth Koch's book inspires young poets to try doing without rhyme, perhaps we should make it available to all of them so that the same thing can happen. Or perhaps we should do more than simply make the book available. Perhaps I should have urged Chelsea more strongly to read that book, or the Williams poems, or even made an assignment out of either or both of them.

It should be clear by now that it would not be my style to choose either of the latter options. But there's more to this issue than style. It's too simple to conclude that Koch's book, in and of itself, was what was inspiring to Chelsea. Nothing this formulaic can fully describe the anatomy of Chelsea's experiment, or tell us why she felt free to make it.

A few months after writing the wine glass poem (which she subsequently revised a bit and titled "At Dinner"), Chelsea sent a poem that she said had been inspired by Arthur Rimbaud's poem "Vowels." "I didn't stick to vowels, though," Chelsea told me.

Here is Rimbaud's poem:

Vowels

Black A, white E, red I, green U, blue O—vowels,
I'll tell, some day, your secret origins:
A, black hairy corset of dazzling flies
Who boom around cruel stenches,

Gulfs of darkness; E, candor of steam and of tents,
Lances of proud glaciers, white kings, Queen-
    Anne's-lace shivers;
I, deep reds, spit blood, laughter of beautiful lips
In anger or in drunkenness and penitence;

U, cycles, divine vibrations of dark green oceans,
Peacefulness of pastures dotted with animals, the
    peace of wrinkles
Which alchemy prints on studious foreheads;

O, supreme trumpet, full of strange harsh sounds,
Silences which are crossed by Worlds and by Angels -
O, Omega, violet ray of Her Eyes! (Koch 1990)

And here is Chelsea's:

Litterarum

The L is white, the precise movements of a geisha's hands,
the folds of a paper crane or snow on bonsai branches.

The S is green, sinuous teasing of grass snakes, the shadow
of a tapir under tree canopies, and olive branches like dead hands.

The T is black, the masks of executioners, large print names
of obscure pompous poets and vagabond rains that wash out
    bridges.

The I is exultation, yellow and pink sunrises, July and flashing
salmon bellies crossing like butter knives.

The Q is grey, the repetitious gossip of red haired women,
a questioning eyebrow on a scholarly face, realistic.

The R is burgundy, libraries, the stained glass windows
of a forgotten church and the sobbing of a bassoon.

Chelsea had read the Rimbaud poem in Kenneth Koch's book, too, so I was curious to see how Koch had used the poem with his students. He had used it with ninth and tenth graders—students the same age as Chelsea, as it happens—as the springboard for an assignment in which students were to "write a poem in which in every line you give the color of a vowel and also mention a few things which have that color. If you like, you can say that these things are the origin of the colors and of the vowels." In explaining this assignment to his students, Koch "went through Rimbaud's poem and made sure they could see each of his color examples clearly,"[8] had them write sample lines, and then let them set to work on writing the longer poems.

I don't know whether Chelsea read Koch's comments or only Rimbaud's poem, but in a sense she enrolled herself in Koch's class by correspondence by setting herself the task he had set his students. Chelsea's experience was not quite the same as the experience of those students, however. Almost as soon as Chelsea decided to try Koch's assignment, it appears, she altered it: "I didn't stick to vowels," she said. Nor did she stick to color images.

There is no question that Rimbaud's poem did inspire Chelsea, that without it "Litterarum," which I consider one of her most successful poems, would not have been written. But unlike Koch's students, Chelsea was not told *how* to make use of "Vowels," how it should inspire her, or even that it should inspire her at all. She was free to use the poem as she wanted to, in the same way that she is free to use everything else she reads (and sees and experiences).

There was no apology in Chelsea's "I didn't stick to vowels, though," but it seems to me that if she had been in Koch's class there might have had to be. Perhaps I'm being unfair to Koch here; I'd like to think that he would be glad to see his students depart from the assignment if what they wrote turned out to be vivid and interesting (or even, perhaps, if it didn't). But it seems to me that if we have a plan for how something ought to inspire someone else, the question then becomes how well they fulfilled that assignment. If they get inspired in another way, or don't get inspired at all, they have to feel guilty, or at least take the trouble to explain why they didn't follow the assignment. I remember sitting in creative writing classes at school and freezing up at assignments that told me how to make use of a particular piece of writing. But I also remember the first time I read a poem about a personal subject, the first time I read a poem written by a woman, the first time I read a poem that didn't capitalize the first word in each line. I was influenced by other people's work, by the possibilities it suggested to me, just as Chelsea was.

We can't mandate exactly how what is read (or seen or experienced) will influence someone else. And yet if children have materials to "appropriate to their own use," as educational theorist Seymour Papert puts it, they may be influenced or inspired by them. The materials can't come with the strings of our expectations attached, though. I *could* have sent Chelsea the Williams poems at any point during our work together, as long as I didn't have any rigid expectations of how she would be affected by them. While I might have sent them to her thinking, "I hope she will see that you don't have to use rhyme," she might have read them and thought, "I didn't realize you could write poems that were addressed directly to other people" or "I didn't know that such simple subjects were acceptable"—or something else entirely.

When I led a writing workshop of homeschoolers years ago, I read them part of W.D. Snodgrass's long poem "Heart's Needle" with the intention of letting them see poetry that was addressed to a particular second person. Although I talked about that before reading the poem, I didn't then assign them the task of writing a poem that used direct address. As a result, some of the children wrote poems during that session that used direct address. Others wrote poems that were clearly influenced by other aspects of Snodgrass's poem—his preoccupation with loss and leaving, for example. And others went about their work without making use (at least at that time) of "Heart's Needle" at all. By reading the poem to the children in that way, I said to them, in effect, "Here's this poem. Make use of it if you want to." Chelsea's family, by leaving Koch's book "lying around," as Chelsea later described it, said the same thing.

To be encouraged to make experiments, then, we often need catalysts—other people, other materials—but we need to be able to use them in ways that make sense to us. I suspect, too, that we need to feel safe enough to take the risk. It's hard, after all, to venture into new territory. I can see that for some, sitting in a classroom with others all writing the same thing could be inspiring. Some of Koch's students may have felt that his telling them to write a particular kind of poem gave them permission, or at least encouragement, to write something that they might not otherwise have dared to write. Yet writers who prefer to work more privately may feel pressured by an assignment and by the prospect of having to show the result to others right away. Perhaps Chelsea felt safer making her experiment in private, and only showing the result when she decided to, than she would have felt in a classroom. Safety will mean different things to different people.

Because of these differences, giving one assignment to a whole group involves a degree of chance: it may be just the catalyst one student needed, but not at all appropriate for another. The only assignments I have ever found useful (and even these were not required) were specific to me and came from someone who knew my work well. Such assignments—but they are really sugges-tions—say, "Given what you're working on, you might want to try this," or "Since you tend to get stuck here, this would probably be good for you to try." I do say these sorts of things to my apprentices. I find it interesting, though, that almost without exception they have never asked for assignments, never said, "Please give me suggestions of things to write about" or anything similar. Some kids probably enjoy this or find it helpful, but it's not the way these particular kids have chosen to use me.

Coming back to Chelsea, I wonder whether she picked up Koch's book specifically hoping to be inspired by it. I would guess not, although I can't be sure. In my experience, it seldom works to sit yourself in front of a particular piece of writing (or experience) and say, "OK, inspire me." The muse, if she exists, is more circuitous and surprising than that. That "popping into your head" that writers marvel at and try so hard to describe (the poet Denise Levertov calls it the "miraculous bird [that has] alighted on your shoulder") cannot be willed, but it can be encouraged, and part of learning how to write is learning what encourages and what discourages inspiration, and how to respond to it when it does come. For example, Kim, at fourteen, wrote in her journal:

> I often get ideas for stories while I'm doing something—most of my inspirations don't come when I'm sitting at the typewriter; most of the time I'm in the middle of something entirely different. Usually it's when I'm doing housework—sweeping, dusting, washing dishes, folding laundry, etc, don't take much concentration. So while I work, I think about all kinds of things (mainly about things I'd rather be doing!), and if I happen to come up with an idea for a story, I stop what I'm doing and write it down. Now I have a drawer with lots of little pieces of paper with descriptions of stories written on them! And also ideas and thoughts about something I'm already writing—if I suddenly think of something like, "Hey, that would be a good addition to my journal," or "I forgot to write about this," or "I need to write a fuller description for that," I write it down so I don't forget. If there's one thing that's really aggravating, it's forgetting a good idea! So I never take a chance, I always write things down. And writing them down means I can file them away and they'll be there till I feel like like working on them—I don't have to focus on them right away.

Kim is the oldest of six children, and in addition to the time she spends on music, dance, and other activities, she has many household responsibilities. There is much that could potentially make it difficult for her to find time to write. But Kim recognizes that writing goes on all the time; though you can't force inspiration to come when you sit down at the typewriter, you can (indeed, must) maintain a kind of perpetual receptivity so that if you get an idea while doing housework, you are ready for it. The fact that Kim stops what she's doing to write down her ideas means that she takes her writing seriously and understands enough about how she works to know that if she didn't write ideas down she would regret it later.

But Kim also gets to decide when to engage in the more focused attentiveness that will turn her ideas into actual stories. She gets to determine how long the interval between inspiration and response will be. Sometimes she may begin work on the story as soon as she's done with the housework and free to concentrate on writing; at other times, she may decide that the idea needs to germinate a while.

When we ask children to read a certain poem and be inspired right then and there, we are ignoring much of what we know about how inspiration actually works. Would a child in a classroom be as free as Kim is to file an idea away until she feels like focusing on it? Or to stop in the middle of something else to write down an idea that has suddenly popped into her head?

But that's real life, people often say to me when I raise these questions. They argue that writers often have to come up with an idea and write something right then and there, and it's good to know how to do that. Furthermore, they say, busy adults can't stop what they're doing to write down ideas as they occur to them. What good does it do to encourage Kim and Chelsea to expect this kind of freedom and control over when they write and don't write if they're soon going to have to learn to do without it?

I happen to think adult writers generally have more control over their lives and work than this suggests. But beyond this, I think that the way Kim and Chelsea have been living and writing up to now is in fact excellent preparation for the time when they may be subject to greater external demands or restrictions. Kim has already shown me this concretely.

She once remarked that my writing life is much more filled with deadlines than hers is. Much of what I write has to be written by a certain time, so that I, more than Kim, *need* to be inspired at particular times. I have had to learn what to do if I can't think of how to approach a piece of writing that must be written soon. I have had to learn how to write for particular audiences, to particular lengths, and so on. Kim has had much less experience with this.

For the first fourteen years of her life, in fact, although she wrote a lot, and in different forms, she never wrote for a deadline, or to anyone else's specifications.

Then I invited her to write for a specific section of *Growing Without Schooling*. Most the the writing in *GWS* is in the form of letters, so the writers have chosen what to write about and when to write it. I'd published excerpts from a few of Kim's letters before, but when she'd written those letters she hadn't originally been writing for publication or for a deadline. But in addition to publishing letters from parents and children, each issue of *GWS* has a section called "Focus," devoted to a particular topic or question. I send out letters inviting people to write for the next issue's Focus, and specifying when I'll need to receive their piece to be able to include it. Readers who choose to write for a particular Focus are accepting a writing assignment, complete with specifications and a firm deadline.

This was a new experience for Kim, and at first it was as hard for her as one might expect. While in the middle of working on it, she wrote to tell me about the trouble she'd been having, and then went on to say:

> I think it's because this is the first time I've ever written anything that I didn't think of myself. I was concentrating too much on the ideas in your letter—to make sure I was writing something that was relevant—and it was like I could only see this certain thing; my brain couldn't think of any new ideas. I'm not saying this is your fault! I shouldn't have used your loose guidelines as the exact example of what I should write. I see that now—but it was hard at the time! . . . Anyway, I was feeling pretty discouraged, because I didn't like what I was writing, and yet I couldn't think of anything else to write. So I talked to Mom. She helped me to really think about what I wanted to say, and how to say it, and how I wasn't saying it. . . . I think I'm doing okay on the piece now, and hope to have it finished soon.

I responded:

> . . . There are in fact real instances in the life of a writer in which you may have to/want to write something with certain kinds of guidelines, and it's good to be able to do that. It

actually gives you *more* freedom, in a funny way, because you can shape what you do, you can *decide* to do something. I hesitate to say that at all because I'm the first to argue that the whole thing involves a delicate balance—sometimes, as you well know, you cannot and should not *will* something to happen in writing. But nevertheless, it seems to me that wanting to write the piece and yet finding it difficult ended up being an interesting challenge for you. . . . I guess a big part of what I'm saying is that hearing how you worked through this actually makes me excited for you because it seems to open up possibilities for you. Now that you know you can do something like this, you can consider writing other kinds of articles or who knows what, in a more focused way. . . .

Kim found it unnerving to have to write to certain specifications and disturbing that writing, which had always come so easily to her, was suddenly so hard. Yet her desire to write—both to write that specific piece and to do what she knew (even before I told her) adult writers often do—made her stick with her experiment.

As it turns out, my hunch was correct; Kim did come through that initial experiment with the ability to write to specifications and with the self-knowledge necessary to do that well. A year or so later, after having written several other such pieces and planning to write more, she told me,

> I'm finding that when I write articles, I have to first think about what things I want to say, and what order they should go in. Then I start with the first one, and think of how I want to say it, and I just keep going through each one that way. The first draft I write is usually pretty rough, and most of the time I write at least three or four more drafts. . . .
>
> The Focus pieces were different from other things I'd written—I had to organize my thoughts before I wrote the actual piece. I had a hard time at first because I didn't realize that I had to do that, that it wasn't like writing the journal, but now I've got it figured out.

This letter confirms what I had said to Kim about the freedom that being able to write to specifications paradoxically gives her. Kim now has the control and the awareness necessary to write organized articles. She can craft and shape her writing with intent, and she has figured out what *she* needs to do to be able to write articles successfully. She is no longer at the mercy of whatever pops into her head; instead of being limited to what she happens to write, she is able to decide what to write, and to accept invitations to write articles for other people. Neither her mother nor I could have told her, "You should organize your thoughts first, and you're going to need to write several drafts," and have expected it to be as effective. Kim had to make that knowledge for herself, out of her own experience.

Incidentally, it may seem as though Kim, in this letter, is contradicting what I said in the previous chapter about writers who think by writing. But in fact I quoted her, in that discussion, describing how rewriting helps her figure out what she thinks about a subject, so that she then has to rewrite the piece yet again to accommodate what she has just learned. When writing articles, she does think before she writes, but she *also* thinks by writing, and that's why her articles go through several drafts.

Writing an organized essay by a particular deadline is something we educators generally want young writers to be able to do. As I said earlier, it may seem as if a young person who was not regularly required, and perhaps even shown how, to write such essays would have a hard time developing the ability. Kim did find it hard at first, but after the initial adjustment she became skilled at it relatively quickly. I think that it was precisely because she had fourteen years of *not* having to write to specifications that she was able to do it so well when she chose to.

It may seem as if the best preparation for something is practice doing that particular thing. It's probably true that the more Kim writes organized essays the better she'll get at it and the easier it will be for her. But Kim's years of self-directed writing gave her other tools that were just as important as regular practice with the actual task of writing to specifications. All those years made Kim comfortable with writing; she had gotten to know it and to know herself, which young people do not always have the chance to do. She had never used writing for any purpose *other* than to say what she wanted to say. It was *hers*, so that when she was faced with the challenge of using it in a new way, she was able, fairly quickly, to figure out what she needed to do. Simple as this sounds, I don't think we can overstate its importance.

We may think that young people who have been required since they were in first grade to finish school assignments by regular deadlines would find meeting real-world deadlines easy and routine. My experience as the editor of my high school newspaper showed me that the opposite was true. Though we had a dedicated core of editors, many of the writers were chronically late with their stories. What struck me was the way in which they would try to negotiate their way out of or around those deadlines, in much the way that we all tried to convince teachers to extend the deadlines for research papers. We were used to deadlines in school, but those deadlines seemed to be the arbitrary decision of one teacher who might be open to persuasion or swayed by a personal excuse. But newspaper deadlines, I remember thinking in frustration, were different. They meant something. The penalty for late school assignments was a lowered grade, unless one could argue one's way out of that. But if a student didn't get an article in on time, lots of other people were prevented from doing lots of other things; the whole process of getting out the paper was held up. It wasn't a matter of convincing me or the other editors to be lenient; the issue wasn't whether we would penalize the students for being late, but the fact that a late story inconvenienced everyone else on the staff, and perhaps even held up the whole issue of the paper. Yet students weren't as familiar with this consequence of being late as they were with the prospect of a lowered grade or a teacher's anger.

The best preparation for meeting real-world writing deadlines, then, is experience with other kinds of real-world deadlines, and experience with using writing for one's own purposes. Kim had had both, so after the initial struggle, she learned (in what was actually a fairly short period of time) how to write an organized essay by a specified time.

Kim's experiment, like Chelsea's, ended up making new things possible. It's interesting that for Chelsea, the experiment involved doing without the rigid specifications she had been accustomed to, while for Kim it involved controlling her writing so that it could fit specifications when she wanted it to. But in both cases, the experiment was liberating. And just as Chelsea now can't imagine not writing unrhymed poetry, Kim now says, "I was thinking about how writing articles is different from writing in the journal, and how I love writing in the journal, but I also need to be writing other things, like the articles." Both Kim and Chelsea have integrated what they learned from these experiments into the whole of their writing lives. I couldn't have known for sure that this would happen, and I certainly couldn't have *made* it happen. But I'm glad I was able to watch it happen. After she'd gotten the letter in which I told her I was excited about how she had figured out how to write the piece for the *GWS* Focus, Kim wrote, "I was thinking how interesting it must be to watch someone else learn and discover things, the way you do with me." Yes, I told her when I wrote again. Yes, it is.

———

SIX

Tools of the Trade

In chapter 3, I quote my friend Katherine saying that what really matters is the work itself, not what mechanisms we use to get it out there. That's why, when I introduced Dory in chapter 4, I said that she wrote her story about the moonlight walk *via dictation*. I purposely put it that way, instead of saying that Dory dictated the story, because I wanted to emphasize Dory's work rather than her method of getting it out there.

I wasn't always this comfortable with seeing dictation as a legitimate form of writing, however. Years ago, when I interviewed Donald Graves about his work with young children, we discussed the place of dictation in a child's development as a writer. Graves was inclined to doubt its value, because he thought that taking dictation discouraged children from feeling fully in charge of their writing and led them to think that "only adults can put words on the page."

I saw his point, and thereafter felt uncomfortable when children asked me to take their dictation, though I never went so far as to refuse them. With a very young child, I feared that my taking dictation was discouraging the child from learning to write things down herself. With an older child, I worried about imposing my own punctuation or paragraphing on the work. Although I would encourage the child to review what I had taken down and make changes freely, I feared that the stylistic decisions I had already made, in the natural course of taking the dictation, might inadvertently influence the writer's decisions when she looked over what we'd done. Above all, I wondered if the activity of dictation, which seemed neither visual nor tactile, could really be considered *writing*.

Several children have since set me straight. Vita, the six-year-old who liked to determine for herself how her mother would help with her writing, responded indignantly to the suggestion that dictating wasn't really writing when she wrote a book review for a national magazine at age fourteen. The book she was reviewing was written by an eleven-year-old girl, with a section written by the girl's younger sister. Vita objected to the parents' having put quotation marks around the word "wrote" when explaining the younger sister's section of the book, as though to imply that she had not really written it because she hadn't put pen to paper. Vita wrote, "It is my opinion that she wrote it as truly as most businessmen and lawyers write their material."

Vita knows that many adults dictate their writing, and when it's all done nobody pays attention to how they got it out there, what particular tool they used. If adults can choose to dictate, why do we worry or consider it less than bona fide when kids do the same thing?

I said that when I was taking the dictation of young children, I worried that I was discouraging them from learning, or even wanting to learn, to write words down themselves. This was foolish of me. If kids see themselves as writers, they will want to do what writers do, and if they don't, they won't (or will think they can't). When I began to pay attention, I saw how dictating actually figured in the lives of the young writers I knew, how it contributed to their growing sense of themselves as writers.

I remembered that Andrea, whose dictated story I mentioned in chapter 2, once showed her mother the transcribed version of that story and told her that she'd written it. "It looks like Susannah's handwriting," said her mother cautiously, and Andrea replied, "Yes, but I wrote it."

She's right. She did write it. Andrea knew what writing something really means, and knew that the story's being in my handwriting didn't make it mine. Furthermore, during this period in her life Andrea was also working at forming words on paper. She knew that that was part of writing too, and gave it a fair share of her attention. So often we think learning happens sequentially—first children dictate, then they learn to write by themselves—when in fact children come at things from all different angles, all at once, sometimes sidling up cautiously, other times rushing in at full tilt. At four, Andrea could dictate a long story that filled two pages of my handwriting, but in the same amount of time could handwrite only a sentence. In time, of course, these things came together for her, so that she no longer needed to dictate to get a whole story written in a reasonable amount of time. But as we know from those "businessmen and lawyers" that Vita referred to, adults don't necessarily give up dictation just because they *can* write or type by themselves. Dictation has its uses even for people older than four-year-olds.

I'll come back to this, but let me introduce one more four-year-old first. Several years ago I lived for a few days with a strong-willed and angry little boy who was generally considered "difficult" by the people around him. He loved to tell stories about Pandy, his stuffed panda bear.

One day when his mother was busy packing for their upcoming move and the boy was being particularly irritating, I said, "Come upstairs with me." "What for?" he asked. "Come with me and see," I suggested. Upstairs, I took out a piece of paper and said, "OK, tell me a Pandy story and I'll write it down." A strange look of fascination came over his face. Did I really mean I would write down whatever he said? He proceeded to tell me a long, detailed story, spilling out words faster than I could get them down. When I had to, I'd stop him and say, "Wait, writing takes longer than talking." He tested me by saying "dirty" words, and I put them in the story like any other words. I wanted to show him that I would indeed write down whatever he said, that he could truly use me to get his story out there and didn't have to worry that I would make any judgments about his language. (This was appropriate because I was acting as a scribe, simply taking down his words. Had he been using me as a critical reader, I might well have offered my opinion about his use of language.)

When he was finished I said, "Should we type it now?" and pointed to the typewriter in the corner. I learned later that he had never seen a typewriter before, but he agreed immediately. I let him turn it on, roll the paper in, set the margin. Then I asked, "Do you want to type the story, or should I?" Again the look of amazement. I could almost see him realize that somehow, in some way he could only just barely glimpse, we were going to *put his words onto that paper* by pressing those buttons. He said, "Me."

I held the sheet with the handwritten story in front of us, and pointed at the keyboard to the first letter, T. He pushed it. I pointed to the next, H. He pushed it. And so we continued for a full paragraph. Each time I asked him if he was growing bored or wanted me to do it he shook his head, no. I wondered if I would have had the patience to do something which was for me so tedious. He didn't know the names of the letters or even, I don't think, that they stand for sounds (though he may have inferred this from our work—I'll never know). There was no way for him to gain typing speed, because he was dependent on me to tell him which letter to push next. And yet he kept at it, pushing each key so gently, with such respect, even grace.

I noticed that after a while he began to be aware of pushing the same key repeatedly, to notice the more common letters. "Why are we pushing these so much?" he asked. "Because your story uses those letters a lot," I told him.

When he finally did grow tired and asked me to type for a while, I said aloud what I was typing, to keep his story in our minds. At one point he asked, "How come I can't do it that fast?" and I replied, "Well, you haven't worked with these letters as long as I have." There was no way to disguise how much faster I was able to type or to pretend that I wasn't the one with the mysterious knowledge of which letter to push, but I tried to make it seem as though this was a simple thing that he too could learn.

From our work I gathered that this boy had not, until that day, thought about getting one of his stories down on paper. Unlike Andrea, he didn't yet see himself as a writer. I hope that after that day he began to. I think his story shows that children can become interested in the writing culture, and welcomed into it by experienced practitioners, long before they put their own words on paper. Dictation was crucial to this boy's early writing experience, as was the experience of using the typewriter. Both were tools. (I suppose you could say that I, as a helpful adult taking down his words, was another kind of tool.) Writers of any age ought to have access to the full range of the trade's tools.

I confirmed for myself that even children who can handwrite fluently benefit from free access to that full range of tools when I was visiting Amanda's family and worked with her on one of her stories. Amanda was eleven at the time, and fully capable of handwriting (or, somewhat more laboriously, typing) her stories, but she often chose dictation as the way of generating her first drafts.

As I typed what Amanda was dictating, I noticed how sensorily rich the activity of dictating actually was, now that I was paying close attention to it. In the course of dictating her story, Amanda moved back and forth between thinking about how the language sounded and thinking about how it looked. Sometimes she would stop and say, "Wait, that doesn't sound right." Other times, when I questioned a choice she had made, she would argue, "But that's how I see it!" Quite often, Amanda spelled out a word as she dictated, not because she thought I didn't know the spelling but because she herself had only read the word, never heard or spoken it. At these times Amanda was clearly thinking visually—seeing in her mind a word that she had once seen on a printed page, and imagining it in her story. At other times, she dictated a word that she had never seen and had no idea how to spell, but chose because it "sounded right."

At frequent intervals—sometimes as often as every other sentence—Amanda came over to the word processor to see how the words looked in type. Although she had a clear picture of the language in her mind, she seemed to need to see it on the screen as well. She would also ask me to read back a sentence or two just to hear the words in another person's voice. Again, both sight and sound were important to her.

Much of the time, Amanda dictated the punctuation herself, relieving me of my worries about the consequences of doing it for her. "Make that a comma," she would say. "No, a dash. Well, what do you think it should be?" In thinking about what it should be, we considered both the rhythm—was it a comma-length or a dash-length pause?—and the look of the sentence on the page.

Even though Amanda's fingers only occasionally touched the keys during the course of her dictation, she was anything but inactive. She paced the room while speaking, and she jumped up and down while resolving some intricacy in plot or wording. In fact, she was rarely still. I can only speculate about how much the suppression of this physical energy might have gotten in the way of her work had she thought that such energy was inappropriate.

Shortly thereafter, I also had occasion to work with Amanda's younger sister, Julia, then six, who asked me to help her write a letter to a pen-pal. Julia was already a proficient sound-speller and kept a journal of her writing; nevertheless, she wanted to dictate the first draft of this letter. (It was she who called it a first draft, demonstrating her familiarity and comfort with the notion of drafts.) I handwrote what Julia dictated, and then she typed up the letter herself, partly for the fun of working the word processor, but also, I imagine, for the sensuality and physicality of making the writing *real*. Finally, she read over the typed letter to see if it looked and sounded the way she wanted it to.

Julia, at six, had read far less than her older sister, so it was not surprising that her ear was stronger than her eye. She could easily tell when something sounded wrong (and yet many older writers have lost this ear for smoothly written language), but she had a more difficult time recognizing an error in spelling or punctuation. Still, she cared about the look of her final letter.

At around the same time, Amanda used dictation to generate the first draft of her homeschooling question-and-answer flyer. This time she used the tape recorder, another useful tool. She recorded her first thoughts about her answers to the questions, and then sent me the tape to transcribe. When I sent the typed version to Amanda, she had a first draft to work with, and she set about adding to it and revising the language, in some places turning spoken language into written, in other places choosing a better word or clarifying her meaning. She changed the sentence, "I do a slide presentation once in a while at conferences" to "I do a slide presentation with my dad when we go to conferences," and changed "Everyone always assumes my mother teaches me" to "Almost everyone assumes my mother teaches me."

From this fine-tuning it's clear that Amanda was sensitive to the nuances of language and to the effect that even a slight alteration had on her meaning. It also confirms, if any doubt remained, that for Amanda the activity of dictating was part of the activity of writing, not a way of avoiding it. Had she simply been talking, or even telling a story, she would not then have gone on to revise, rearrange, and expand in the same way. If I had taken down on paper, without her being aware of it, a story she had told aloud, it wouldn't be accurate to say that she had dictated that story. Dictation, as I'm using it here, refers to the activity of speaking aloud as part of working on a piece of writing. It implies intent to generate written material in a way that speaking while someone happens to be taking down your words does not.

If we think dictation is only a prelude to writing, or a distraction from it, just because it doesn't *seem* like writing, we discourage both young children and older children from making full use of it as a tool. "Now that you can write yourself, you don't have to dictate anymore," we might say to a child, thinking of this as a cause for celebration. Well, children probably do feel liberated by not *having* to dictate; learning to handwrite gives them new options, as does learning how to type. But they shouldn't have to give up one tool just because they learn to use another. Tools best serve *any* writer if they can be used flexibly. Chelsea, telling me that she now uses the computer frequently for revising and sometimes for composing first drafts, added that she continues to handwrite often and that "sometimes switching back and forth between handwriting and typing can get me out of a rut."

The word processor is considered a boon to writers because of all the retyping it saves. That's often true. But I have been known to print out a draft, read it over, and then retype the whole thing in a new file and in the process make the changes that turn it into the second draft. Now that I use a computer I shouldn't have to retype anymore, just as a child who can handwrite shouldn't have to dictate. But sometimes I choose to retype, because I think with my fingers on the keyboard. My particular way of working means that I sometimes want to retype even though I technically don't have to, and another writer's way of working may mean that she will choose to dictate even when she has other tools available.

My particular style, by the way, probably also explains my initial reluctance to appreciate the uses of dictation. I couldn't imagine dictating precisely because the physical act of writing is so much a part of the process for me. And, of course, some young writers may also feel as I do. Chelsea told me, "I used to dictate some things to my mother but I haven't for a long time. I need to see the writing itself and to actually be putting it down to do it best." Chelsea prefers other tools, and that's fine. Nothing I've said about dictating implies that because it is useful to some it must be useful to all. My point is only that it is as legitimate as any writing tool.

Sometimes our assumptions about a particular tool are what unnecessarily restrict us (computers mean you shouldn't retype; dictation means you aren't putting words down on paper). Other times our assumptions about how people behave at various ages do it instead. We may think that a child is too old for dictating but too young to use the computer, thereby eliminating two of his most flexible and versatile options. If children have a range of tools at their disposal, and no prejudices about their legitimacy or (as the jargon has it) age-appropriateness, we don't have to worry if they don't approach these tools in a linear, sequential way.

Simply not knowing how to use a tool can be limiting. Mika told me that she seldom revises the stylistic and grammatical components of her fiction because she doesn't know how to type and doing the job in handwriting seems overwhelming. She is looking forward to the day that her family gets a computer, and she expects to spend more time revising her stories then. Kim, too, was stymied at the thought of revising her education journal (which is a book-length manuscript) until she gained access to a computer and learned how to use it. Some might argue that no writer should depend so heavily on any one tool. To some extent, I agree. But that's all the more reason not to restrict ourselves, or our children, by keeping some tools off limits. The more we know how to and feel allowed to use, the more options we have. More tools make more things possible.

―――

SEVEN

Blocks and Periods of Not Writing

My favorite of the ubiquitous "light bulb" jokes is the one that goes, "How many Zen Buddhists does it take to change a light bulb?" "Two," is the answer. "One to change the light bulb, and one *not* to change the light bulb." I like the idea that the not-doing is in some way as essential to the task as the doing of it. We need the explicit action, but we also need the counterpart, or underside, of non-action.

How many writers does it take to complete a given piece of work? The activity of writing, too, has its counterpart, or complement, of not-writing. The dry periods, the thinking-before-writing, the taking time away from a piece to let it gel—all these are part of the activity, and yet when we think about appropriate conditions for writing—particularly children's writing—we often forget to figure this in.

Just after Kim turned fourteen she wrote to me:

> I haven't done any writing (other than letters or in my diary) for about a week now, because I felt my brain was being drained. I'd been writing intensely for a month or so, and I was beginning to feel like my brain had had all the thought thought out of it! Sometimes you have to step back and forget about the things you're writing for a while, and then when you come back, you're able to look at them with a fresh perspective. It's been tough, though, keeping myself from

writing, because I'm just dying to work on my newest ideas. That's the way I always feel when I have a new idea that's exciting and that interests me. But I've made myself do other things because even though I really do want to write, I know I'm still not ready to start up again yet. I'm just resting now, kind of like I'm storing up fresh energy and enthusiasm.

Some might protest that letters and diaries are certainly writing. How can Kim say she hasn't been writing for a week, and dismiss so parenthetically what is probably more writing than many others would do in the same amount of time? Kim does know that letters and diaries are legitimate forms of writing. The project to which she's devoted most of her energy for the past year is, as I've said, written in journal form. But I think many writers would laugh with recognition at Kim's distinction between writing in which she is consciously making something (stories and articles) and writing that she does more routinely, in the course of being alive (letters and her diary). It's not that one is better than the other, but, perhaps that one is Kim's primary work and the other is what serves that work. She may write letters or diary entries as a way of formulating her thoughts for a story or article, but neither a letter nor a diary entry *is* the story or article. One is the material; the other is what is made out of the material.

In any case, what is important here is that Kim felt it was necessary to take time away from writing, and felt that that was what she was doing. This is what I focused my attention on as I thought about how to respond.

I could understand Kim's need to take time away from a piece of work so as to be able to come back to it with a fresh perspective, but the idea that she kept herself from writing even when she had plenty to say and wanted to write struck me, at the time, as unusual and intriguing. Writers often talk themselves into putting a piece of writing aside for a while when it's giving them trouble, when they're stuck and see taking a break as the only solution. But Kim seemed to be talking about something else. She was keeping herself from writing not when she was stuck but when she was full of ideas that excited and interested her. Was this necessary? I wondered. Wasn't there a danger that those ideas would get old and suffer from Kim's inattention to them, so that they would eventually be harder to write?

I wrote to Kim:

I was very interested in your explanation of your writing process, and how you sometimes have to keep yourself from writing. It's funny, because when I'm not writing it tends not to be because I've chosen not to, but because I'm blocked in some way, so it doesn't have that feeling of, "I could write right now, but I think I won't." I'm interested in pushing you a little further on this question by saying, how do you know it's necessary to keep yourself from writing when you clearly do have the energy to do it, and the ideas? What do you think would happen if you did write when you felt "full" like that?

She responded:

You said that when you don't write, it's because you're blocked in some way. This "burn out" is really kind of a block too. I would have ideas of what I wanted to write, but when I'd try to write, it seemed like my brain just sort of shut down, it was too tired. So I'd get frustrated because I wasn't writing the way I wanted to. I guess I was beginning to feel that if I didn't get all my thoughts on paper right away, they would vanish. Now I'm more relaxed. I've told myself, "Quit worrying, you'll still be able to get fresh, new inspiration for more stories, and for the ones you're already working on." I've had about one month off from writing, and I'm ready to get back to it.

So it *was* originally a feeling of stuckness that kept Kim from writing. She took time off as a way to cope with that feeling, but, apparently, something told her to hold off a little longer, to wait even when the ideas began to build up again. Like Virginia Woolf, who said, "As for my next book, I am going to hold myself from writing it till I have it impending in me: grown heavy in my mind like a ripe pear; pendant, gravid, asking to be cut or it will fall,"[9] Kim chose to wait until the ideas welled up in her and demanded to be written.

I am struck here, as I am by so many of the things my apprentices do, by Kim's ability to figure out for herself how she needed to respond to a particular situation, unhampered by others' expectations. And because she responded by spending some time away from writing, Kim taught me (or, at least, reminded me of) something that I could not have learned if she were working under other circumstances.

Kim took her freedom to decide not to write for granted. Because she was able to choose not to write when that was what she needed, I, in turn, was able to learn *when* not-writing was necessary to her. I could see how she used it and begin to think about how others use it. If Kim had not been able to take that month away from writing, neither she nor I would have learned what we did.

Kim figured out that even though a writing block involves not being able to write, sometimes not writing is the cure as well. But Kim's resistance to writing even when she felt full of ideas and eager to write suggests that resistance, or holding back, has its place in the scheme of things even when being blocked or stuck is not the issue.

Donald Murray writes in *Learning by Teaching*: "Teachers and writers too often consider resistance to writing evil, when, in fact, it is necessary. When I get an idea for a poem or an article or a talk or a short story, I feel myself consciously draw away from it. I seek procrastination and delay. There must be time for the seed of the idea to be nurtured in the mind." And later he adds, "Often I write by not writing. I assign a task to my subconscious, then take a nap or go for a walk, do errands, and let my mind work on the problem."[10]

The business of assigning a task to the subsconscious is very familiar to me, and Murray makes me realize that even when I originally responded to Kim I understood her decision better than I thought I did. At the time, I had been focusing on the feeling of "nothing coming" and had wondered why Kim would choose not to write when she had so much in her head, instead of feeling grateful for being so full. But in fact I, too, often "write by not writing."

Kim's story is not only about choosing not to write, though. As her second letter suggests, it's also about figuring out when it's time to write again. When I was in college the poet and novelist Margaret Atwood visited and spent time with a small group of students. When one student asked a question that had to do with a poem she just couldn't get right, Atwood said, "It could be that you wrote it down too soon." How could Kim tell when it was safe to go back to writing? How does Donald Murray know how long to resist, to seek procrastination and delay? These questions aren't easy, and they can't be answered by an externally imposed routine that tells us when we will write and when we will move on to something else.

Virginia Woolf planned to wait until the urgency of her book, the ripeness, left no doubt in her mind about its readiness to be written. Kim set herself a specific amount of time during which she wouldn't write, but she, too, waited until the urgency built up again. And now Kim knows how to use these periods of not writing when she feels the need.

It's because Kim knows this that her need to take time off from writing is not incompatible with writing to specific deadlines. I described in chapter 5 how Kim learned what meeting deadlines involved and how to adapt her own work to fit inside that frame. We figure out what we need to do and then allow time to do it, and needing to take time away from a piece is no exception. I know that even when I'm writing to a tight deadline I have to take into account my need to spend some time away from the piece. Each issue of *Growing Without Schooling,* for example, has a front-page essay that I must write, and that I write at the last minute, after all the other material is in. I make sure to write the essay at least one day before it's time to lay out the issue, so that it can sit overnight and I can look at it again the next day. With other types of work, I allow for a much longer period of time away, or, more commonly, several cycles of time away and time at work on the piece—but of course I'm always at work on it, as Donald Murray so aptly points out. Again, knowing these things about my own working process means that I can allow for them and still meet deadlines. And so can Kim. But the self-knowledge had to come first.

Of course, neither Kim nor I would be honest if we didn't admit that we have to learn about the rhythms of writing and not-writing over and over again. It's almost as if writing teaches us about our processes each time we involve ourselves in it. Recently, over two years after her initial experience with not-writing, Kim wrote about an article she was working on: "It's funny, but half of the work of writing doesn't happen on paper, but in my head. . . . As many times as I've gone through this process, I'm still impatient and reluctant when I get to the point where I need to let the article be." It's hard to resist, to remember what worked last time and to believe it will work again. It's just as hard for me, sometimes, to let go of that perfect piece of writing in my head and let it fall, flawed but now accessible to readers, onto the page. If I keep it in my head and never write it down, it remains the ideal piece of writing that I aspire to, but no one else can read it and so it never exists as something real and in the world. If I write it down, it becomes a draft, now imperfect and demanding to be worked on. But it's real and exists out there, not just in my head, so I decide it's worth the loss.

I've been talking here about situations in which we *choose* not to write. But what about those times when we want to write and the writing doesn't come? This is really what I was wondering about when I wrote that letter to Kim. How can we tell when we're not writing for good and ultimately productive reasons, and when we're not writing because we're blocking ourselves or can't think of what to say or aren't giving our writing a high enough priority in our lives?

Chelsea, explaining in one letter that she hadn't written any poems recently, said, "My writing bug is sort of dormant right now." Writers differ in their ability to handle such dormancy. Some accept it calmly and happily go about other activities. Others worry that this is it; they've written their last word. Some people try various schemes to entice the muse to deliver something.

Here is Donald Murray again:

> The writing is going well. Everything is connecting. I need a word, and it is in my ear; I need a fact, and it flows out of my fingers; I need a more effective order, and my eye watches sentences as they rearrange themselves on the page. I think this is what writing should be like, and then I stop. I go for another mug of coffee, visit the bathroom, check the mail.
>
> I wonder about this compulsion to interrupt writing which is going well. I see my students do it in the writing workshop. It's so much of a pattern that there must be a reason for it. Sometimes I think it is the workman's need to stand back to get distance; other times I think it is simple Calvinist distrust—when everything's going well, something must be wrong.[11]

If I were looking for an example of a writer writing about his own work in a way that resonated with my own experience, I couldn't find a better one than this passage of Murray's. I know exactly what he means. I especially love the way Murray admits that he doesn't know whether this particular kind of not-writing is good or bad. Would it be better for him (or any of us) to push his way through that impulse to stop writing, and so learn to trust the work when it's going well and to withstand those moments of restlessness and doubt? Or is the impulse saying something important that Murray should heed? I don't know. All I know is that we have to figure out for ourselves what to do about this impulse, and we may never figure it out completely.

The self-knowledge Kim gained from taking time away from a piece of writing now seems to be an integral part of her writing life. Often these days she tells me about how she isn't working on something now but will be soon, or was working on it but is now taking a break. But remember Mika, in chapter 3, whose experience with how hard it was to get back to writing after time away from it taught her that she needed to write every day. Mika experienced that rustiness as a problem, so she developed a way to solve it. Kim had a different problem and a different solution. Furthermore, what one writer perceives as a problem—the fact of not having written for a while, for example—another may accept as normal and even healthy. Chelsea had to decide whether it bothered her that she hadn't been writing any poems lately, and if it did, what to do about it. Watching my apprentices decide how to handle being blocked or stuck means watching them decide, first of all, whether they *are* stuck, and then, afterwards, figure out what to do about it. By watching them I gain a better sense of the options writers have.

Amanda, at ten, told me that she was putting one story aside for a while because being stuck on one of the points of its plot was making her feel stuck about all her stories, and she didn't want that to happen. She decided to take time away, not from writing in general, but from the writing of one specific story, so as to protect the rest of her writing. Instead of letting that one story stand as a roadblock to any future writing, she said to herself, "Never mind; I'll go around it and maybe come back to it later."

Similarly, when I conducted a writing workshop for a group of children at a homeschooling conference, I asked the children if they had any questions they wanted to ask each other about long-term projects that they were involved in. These kids hadn't been in a workshop before, and I said that perhaps they were facing specific challenges in the course of working on their own and would like to ask others for suggestions while they had the chance.

One girl volunteered immediately, saying that she was working on a play and was having trouble beginning it. She knew what she wanted it to be about, she said, but she didn't know how to write the opening scene. Right away another child had an idea. "I think you should start with the scene you're thinking of," he suggested. "Write the one that made you think of the play, and then you can go back and do the beginning later. That's what I do when I'm stuck like that." Don't let being stuck about one part force you to be stuck about the whole thing, this boy was saying, much as Amanda had advised herself.

These kids' drive to figure out ways to get over or under or around various writing blocks indicates the strength of their determination, or how deeply they feel themselves to be writers in the first place. This is what made Amanda concerned about protecting the rest of her writing, what made Kim have to devise a careful plan that would allow her energy and enthusiasm to build up again, and what makes all the kids' not-writing time very much a part of their writing lives.

A couple of years ago I went through a long period of not writing poems. I hadn't chosen it, didn't enjoy it, and wasn't sure what had caused it. Periodically I tried to do something about it. But it never crossed my mind that I might have stopped writing poems forever. Right in the middle of this difficult period I heard someone say, "I used to write poems, but I don't anymore," and I realized how I knew I was blocked rather than simply finished with poetry: I couldn't say the same thing. I couldn't just let it go. Even when I felt most hopeless about poetry, I never truly stopped working, never stopped figuring out how to work through the block and get back to writing again.

We hold ourselves to high standards, perhaps with good reason. When I am making excuses not to write, or simply finding it difficult to clear a space for writing in the midst of other things, I sometimes say to myself in disgust, "A writer is one who writes, and if you don't get busy, you have no right to call yourself a writer." I never want to be someone who talks endlessly about writing, cultivates the writer persona, without actually writing anything. But if I'm honest with myself I know, as Kim and the others know, that periods of not-writing can be essential and don't mean that I'm not still hard at work.

We tend to have even less tolerance for not-writing in young writers. If children stop writing, we are much more inclined to think that they've given it up for good. Naturally we have to be alert to the signals children send out: it may indeed be that something has happened to turn the child off, made her afraid or made her see her abilities in the wrong light. I wouldn't just let it go if a child mistook spelling for writing, for example, and thought that she couldn't write because she was a poor speller. I wouldn't just let it go if a child took a rejection notice too hard, or for some other reason decided that she *couldn't* write. Of course we want to be sensitive to the sort of discouragement or frustration that we can do something about. But children, like adults, deserve to be able to think of themselves as writers even when they are not actively producing something. If years go by between one novel and another, we don't immediately assume that an adult novelist has taken up a new vocation. We accept that all sorts of work may be going on under the surface, work that may reveal itself in surprising ways when the writing does come again. The same can be true for child writers.

I was lucky to have found a teacher who was truly helpful to me just before I entered into my long dry period. I say I was lucky because even though I sometimes felt foolish for having found a teacher and then promptly ceasing to write, I knew that the teacher would be there when I began writing again. I knew that she, being a writer herself, would understand about dry spells. (Of course, she would have understood, too, if it had been circumstances in my life as a whole, rather than circumstances in my writing life, that had made me stop taking advantage of her help. Adults have more freedom than kids generally do to say, "I've been busy with other things," or to stop something with no explanation at all.)

Remembering how helpful I found that teacher's unconditional availability, I try to communicate the same acceptance to my apprentices by reminding them (sometimes several times) that they have no obligation to use me with any regularity, and, even more important, that if they don't send me any work for months and then want to again, I'll be available to them without judgment. Just recently I heard from a young writer whom I hadn't heard from in over a year. I was glad that she felt free to work with me again after so much time had elapsed. Of course, I don't communicate indifference; I don't imply that it makes no difference to me whether I ever hear from them again. My interest in their work is apparent, and I always let them know that I'm glad to hear from them again, am curious to see what they've been working on, and so on. But I never say, "Why haven't you been writing?" or "Why haven't you been sending me what you've written?" Perhaps knowing that they can send me work even after long intervals have passed reminds the kids that I think of them as writers regardless of how much writing they produce during any given period, or how much of it I ever see. I would like to think so.

Devotion to the Work

Throughout this book I have found myself coming again and again to the question of vocation, or how the kids' devotion to writing feeds the work they do. Of all the ways that I am saying young writers can be like adult writers, this one seems to me most important. Yet it is easy to forget or to misunderstand.

One of the most popular words in education is "motivation." We may not be sure how to get it or what it would look like, but we sense that if kids had it, many educational problems would take care of themselves. Given the circumstances under which we usually see children, though, it's almost impossible to believe that motivation could be something kids have even *before* we try to give it to them.

The one creative writing course my high school offered—an elective course—was billed as one in which assignments would not be graded. Halfway through the year, however, the teacher announced that henceforth all our work would receive traditional letter grades. "I'm sorry to have to do this," she said, "but I can't see how else to get you to do the work." We are so used to setting our dealings with young people in a carrot-and-stick framework that even when we try to frame them another way, we retreat back into the familiar territory of rewards and punishments at the slightest discomfort or failure. This teacher's inability, or refusal, to think about motivation in any but the most traditional way cost her whatever opportunity she might have had in that classroom to understand how we really worked and what we wanted from her.

The other side of artificial motivation, of course, is artificial punishment or deterrent. My ninth-grade math teacher announced at the start of the year that he would deduct five points from the final grade of students who wrote on their desks. "I hate to have to do it," he told us, "but I can't think of any other way to make sure that you don't write on the desks."

No other way? Is there really nothing else we can appeal to in young people but their fear of punishment or hope of reward? Suppose that instead of asking himself, "What kind of penalty can I impose to deter the students from writing on the desks?" this teacher had asked, "How can I strengthen my students' relationship to the school, or at least to this classroom, so that they would no more think of writing on the desks than they would think of mistreating anything else they valued?" The array of possible answers would have been transformed, as it would have been for the creative writing teacher had she not immediately and inextricably linked motivation with grades and thus stopped thinking about how else to foster it. Deeply embedded in and crucial to our relationships with young people are these attitudes about them and the work they do. If we think of young people as motivated or deterred only by grades or other external means, if we cannot imagine any other reason for them to engage in serious work, then all my descriptions of the young writers in this book seem improbable or nonsensical. To understand them, we have to think about young people, and indeed about work itself, in another way.

Poet and essayist Annie Dillard writes:

> There's a common notion that discipline is a freakish peculiarity of writers—that writers differ from other people by possessing enormous and equal portions of talent and willpower. They grit their powerful teeth and go into their little rooms. I think that's a bad misunderstanding of what impels the writer. What impels the writer is a deep love of and respect for language, for literary forms, for books. It's a privilege to be able to muck about in sentences all morning. It's a challenge to bring off a powerful effect, or to tell the truth about something. You don't do it from willpower; you do it from an abiding passion for the field. . . .

Writing a book is like rearing children—willpower has very little to do with it. If you have a little baby crying in the middle of the night, and if you depend only on willpower to get you out of bed to feed the baby, that baby will starve. You do it out of love. Willpower is a weak idea; love is strong. You don't have to scourge yourself with a cat-o'-nine-tails to go to the baby. You go to the baby out of love for that particular baby. That's the same way you go to your desk. There's nothing freakish about it. Caring passionately about something isn't against nature, and it isn't against human nature. It's what we're here to do. [12]

Of course, sometimes we go to our desks for other reasons: perhaps out of vanity, or habit, or obligation. Sometimes we may fear our work, or resent it, or simply grow tired of it. But if our work is real, and enduring, and truly ours, then at the center of it *is* the love, the devotion, that Annie Dillard writes about. For people unfamiliar with the feeling, this may be hard to believe, and it is even harder to believe that young people can go to their desks out of the same motivation.

Many things we try to "get" children to do are things that they would do anyway, without any artificial urging, as long as they first had the opportunity for the necessary devotion to take hold. When we love a baby, says Annie Dillard, there is no end to what we will do for it, and we don't need to summon willpower in order to make ourselves do it. When we are devoted to our writing, we will revise a piece because we want it to be clearer and sound better; we will negotiate our way around writing blocks because we can't imagine being finished with writing forever; we will involve other people in our work because we value the help and the critical response they give us. This is no less true for children than it is for adults.

If we love something, we will work for it and learn it. Loving is where it begins, not where it ends; my apprentices don't sit around loving writing but not working at it or sticking with it when it gets hard. Ami said, "I'm pretty devoted to my writing and want to find ways to improve it." The devotion gives rise to the work; it's what makes it worth doing.

When I talk about these kids to people I know, some listeners can't get past the simple fact that they do work hard at their writing without any of the usual carrots or sticks spurring them on. This alone seems remarkable. Why would Kim have written a thirty-page, single-spaced story before she began working with me if no one required it and she couldn't be sure anyone was going to see it? Why would Mika decide to write every day? Why would Ariel revise a private diary? Again and again these kids demonstrate that there are reasons for doing these things other than obligation or fear or hope of reward. And in fact, if we adults have work that we love, we know about those other reasons, have felt them ourselves. The surprise from an educational point of view is that children can feel them too.

Talk about education doesn't need to be talk only about how to motivate or entice or impel; it can also be about the conditions under which devotion and a sense of workmanship will flourish. That is why it's important to look at the circumstances of the working lives of children who feel these things. George Dennison, author of *The Lives of Children*, said in an unpublished transcript of a discussion about freedom in education:

> Once you start looking for freedom, you're lost. Can you imagine finding it? Hey, here's freedom! Over here! Look! But all you can see, you know, is people doing things. What we mean is we're not going to coerce anybody, either by force or cunning. . . .
>
> But the absence of coercion isn't visible either. What's visible, when things are going well, is simply activities, activities of all kinds, especially, we hope, the kinds that harmonize energy, innate powers, and sweet reason. The real touchstone of freedom, you know, is not joyous people romping in the grass, but quality, first-rate work. . . . You don't reach this by regimenting people, or by having a *lifestyle* of freedom— which tends to be all style and no life—but by doing things, especially the things you can do with a whole heart.

And sometimes, for some people, for a variety of reasons both accidental and intentional, writing will be one of the things they do with a whole heart. Of all that I have learned from the kids I work with, I have learned the most from seeing this in them, and from remembering how it grew in my own childhood.

I learned about devotion in myself from seeing it in another. One of the first things I learned about Lydia, my best friend during my fourth-grade year, was that she got up at five every morning and read until it was time to get ready for school. I learned this months before Lydia and I fully became friends, and yet I marveled at it: here was someone who loved what I loved more than I loved it, and who was willing to support that love with dedication, to insist on making room for it no matter what else her life required of her.

Later, when we were writing stories together, Lydia came to school one morning having written forty pages in a night. I was impressed by the volume, but I was even more impressed by what it stood for: a luxury of devotion, an ability to take one's love for words and go with it as far as it was possible to go. Stunned by Lydia's excess, or discipline, I was also stunned by my own desire, at nine years old, to match it. In Lydia's devotion I saw myself, saw what I was and what I wanted.

When our class went on trips to the museum, to the United Nations, I don't think Lydia and I heard a word of what went on. We used that time (time school seldom otherwise gave us) to talk about our latest stories—or books, as we ambitiously called them. I realize now how much we relied on the inspiration we gave each other. Some writers say talking about a book distracts you from writing it, and perhaps our books were never finished because we talked so much, and so excitedly, about what was going to go in them. But the miracle at that time was having someone else as busy thinking of a good title for your work as you were, someone you could call on the phone the moment you figured out what was going to happen to your central character. We were for each other the kind of guaranteed, steady readers that adult writers dream of. "I bet Lydia will say no one talks like that," I would say to myself, already imagining ways to revise the line. "Oh, this is great! I can't wait to show this to Lydia tomorrow!" I'd exclaim, allowing my private jubilation the company of an anticipated reader, welcoming the change from writing's usual solitude. To this day I experience writing as both solitary and inextricably bound up with other people—teachers, readers, colleagues. With Lydia I learned about my own private devotion *and* about how to involve someone else in it, much as I see my apprentices learning now.

Devotion, as I've said, is not the only thing. It's the beginning. We have to think about how to make a life that will serve that devotion. We struggle with finding the right teachers, understanding ourselves well enough to know what we need to do, working through difficult periods. My apprentices struggle with these things now, as children and teenagers, and they will struggle with them in new and perhaps sometimes more problematic ways as they get older. I, in turn, will always struggle with how best to help them, how to respond appropriately, meaningfully, and in ways that they can truly use. But I cannot dismiss as trivial the exuberance, the immersion, that I learned from Lydia and am seeing all over again in the young people I work with now. I know there is something central to my adult work that has its roots in that early time, something that draws its sustenance from the knowledge that was attained then, knowledge that expresses itself simply as: this is yours.

Notes

1. Frank Smith, *Insult to Intelligence* (Portsmouth, NH: Heinemann Educational Books, 1986), 62.

2. David Deutsch, "How Children Can Become Experts," *Growing Without Schooling* 29 (10/82): 11–12.

3. Herbert Kohl, *The Question Is College* (New York: Random House, 1989), 69.

4. In Smith, *Insult to Intelligence*, 40.

5. Nancy Wallace, "Rethinking the Teacher's Red Ink," *Growing Without Schooling* 69 (6/89): 10.

6. Donald M. Murray, *Shoptalk* (Portsmouth, NH: Boynton/Cook, 1990), 8.

7. Nancy Wallace, *Child's Work* (Cambridge, MA: Holt Associates, 1990), 117.

8. Kenneth Koch, *Rose, Where Did You Get That Red?* (New York: Vintage Books, 1990), 162–4.

9. Virginia Woolf, *A Writer's Diary* (New York: Harcourt Brace Jovanovich, 1953), 136.

10. Donald M. Murray, *Learning by Teaching* (Portsmouth, NH: Boynton/Cook, 1982), 33.

11. Murray, *Learning by Teaching*, 43.
12. Annie Dillard, "To Fashion a Text," in William Zinsser, ed., *Inventing the Truth: The Art and Craft of Memoir* (Boston: Houghton Mifflin, 1987), 75–6.